Asbestos Standard for the Construction Industry and Lead in Construction

OSHA

Government Institutes
An imprint of
The Scarecrow Press, Inc.
Lanham, Maryland • Toronto • Plymouth, UK
2008

Government Institutes

Published in the United States of America
by Government Institutes, an imprint of The Scarecrow Press, Inc.
A wholly owned subsidiary of
The Rowman & Littlefield Publishing Group, Inc.
4501 Forbes Boulevard, Suite 200
Lanham, Maryland 20706
http://www.govinstpress.com/

Estover Road
Plymouth PL6 7PY
United Kingdom

Asbestos Standard for the Construction Industry

OSHA 3096

2002 (Revised)

This informational book provides a generic, non-exhaustive overview of a particular topic related to OSHA standards. It does not alter or determine compliance responsibilities in OSHA standards or the *Occupational Safety and Health Act of 1970*. Because interpretations and enforcement policy may change over time, you should consult current administrative interpretations and decisions by the Occupational Safety and Health Review Commission and the Courts for additional guidance on OSHA compliance requirements.

This information is available to sensory impaired individuals upon request.
Voice phone: (202) 693-1999; Teletypewriter (TTY) number: (877) 889-5627.

∞™ The paper used in this publication meets the minimum requirements of American National Standard for Information Sciences—Permanence of Paper for Printed Library Materials, ANSI/NISO Z39.48-1992.
Manufactured in the United States of America.

ISBN: 978-0-86587-521-0

Summary Contents

Contents

Asbestos Standard for the Construction Industry

Introduction

What is asbestos?

Asbestos is the generic term for a group of naturally occurring, fibrous minerals with high tensile strength, flexibility, and resistance to heat, chemicals, and electricity.

In the construction industry, asbestos is found in installed products such as sprayed-on fireproofing, pipe insulation, floor tiles, cement pipe and sheet, roofing felts and shingles, ceiling tiles, fire-resistant drywall, drywall joint compounds, and acoustical products. Because very few asbestos containing products are being installed today, most worker exposures occur during the removal of asbestos and the renovation and maintenance of buildings and structures containing asbestos.

What are the dangers of asbestos exposure?

Asbestos fibers enter the body when a person inhales or ingests airborne particles that become embedded in the tissues of the respiratory or digestive systems. Exposure to asbestos can cause disabling or fatal diseases such as asbestosis, an emphysema-like condition; lung cancer; mesothelioma, a cancerous tumor that spreads rapidly in the cells of membranes covering the lungs and body organs; and gastrointestinal cancer. The symptoms of these diseases generally do not appear for 20 or more years after initial exposure.

What construction activities does this book cover?

The asbestos standard for the construction industry (29 CFR Part 1926.1101, see www.osha.gov) regulates asbestos exposure for the following activities:

- Demolishing or salvaging structures where asbestos is present.
- Removing or encapsulating asbestos-containing material (ACM).
- Constructing, altering, repairing, maintaining, or renovating asbestos-containing structures or substrates.
- Installing asbestos-containing products.
- Cleaning up asbestos spills/emergencies.
- Transporting, disposing, storing, containing, and housekeeping involving asbestos or asbestos-containing products on a construction site.

Note: The standard does not apply to asbestos-containing asphalt roof coatings, cements, and mastics.

Provisions of the OSHA Standard

OSHA has established strict exposure limits and requirements for exposure assessment, medical surveillance, recordkeeping, ***competent persons***, regulated areas, and hazard communication.

What is work classification?

The OSHA standard establishes a classification system for asbestos construction work that spells out mandatory, simple, technological work practices that employers must follow to reduce worker exposures. Under this system, the following four classes of construction work are matched with increasingly stringent control requirements:

- ***Class I*** asbestos work is the most potentially hazardous class of asbestos jobs. This work involves the removal of asbestos-containing thermal system insulation and sprayed-on or troweled-on surfacing materials. Employers must presume that thermal system insulation and surfacing material found in pre-1981 construction is ACM. That presumption, however, is rebuttable. If you believe that the surfacing material or thermal system insulation is not ACM, the OSHA standard specifies the means that you must use to rebut that presumption. Thermal system insulation includes ACM applied to pipes, boilers, tanks, ducts, or other structural components to prevent heat loss or gain. Surfacing materials include decorative plaster on ceilings and walls; acoustical materials on decking, walls, and ceilings; and fireproofing on structural members.
- ***Class II*** work includes the removal of other types of ACM that are not thermal system insulation such as resilient flooring and roofing materials. Examples of Class II work include removal of asbestos-containing floor or ceiling tiles, siding, roofing, or transite panels.
- ***Class III*** asbestos work includes repair and maintenance operations where ACM or presumed ACM (PACM) are disturbed.
- ***Class IV*** work includes custodial activities where employees clean up asbestos-containing waste and debris produced by construction, maintenance, or repair activities. This work involves cleaning dust-contaminated surfaces, vacuuming contaminated carpets, mopping floors, and cleaning up ACM or PACM from thermal system insulation or surfacing material.

What is the permissible exposure limit for asbestos?

Employers must ensure that no employee is exposed to an airborne concentration of asbestos in excess of 0.1 f/cc as an 8-hour time-weighted average (TWA). In addition, employees must not be exposed to an airborne concentration of asbestos in excess of 1 f/cc as averaged over a sampling period of 30 minutes.

Which asbestos operations must employers monitor and assess?

Employers must assess all asbestos operations for the potential to generate airborne fibers, and use exposure monitoring data to assess employee exposures. You must also designate a *competent person* to help ensure the safety and health of your workers.

What is the function of a *competent person*?

On all construction sites with asbestos operations, employers must designate a *competent person*—one who can identify asbestos hazards in the workplace and has the authority to correct them. This person must be qualified and authorized to ensure worker safety and health as required by *Subpart C, General Safety and Health Provisions for Construction* (29 CFR Part 1926.20). Under these requirements for safety and health prevention programs, the *competent person* must frequently inspect job sites, materials, and equipment.

The *competent person* must attend a comprehensive training course for contractors and supervisors certified by the U.S. Environmental Protection Agency (EPA) or a state approved training provider, or a complete a course that is equivalent in length and content.

For *Class III and IV* asbestos work, training must include a course equivalent in length, stringency, and content to the 16-hour *Operations and Maintenance* course developed by EPA for maintenance and custodial workers. For more specific information, see 40 CFR Part 763.92(a)(2).

What is an initial exposure assessment?

To determine expected exposures, a *competent person* must perform an initial exposure assessment to assess exposures immediately before or as the operation begins. This person must perform the assessment in time to comply with all standard requirements triggered by exposure data or the lack of a negative exposure assessment and to provide the necessary information to ensure all control systems are appropriate and work properly. A negative exposure assessment demonstrates that employee exposure during an operation is consistently below the permissible exposure limit (PEL).

The initial exposure assessment must be based on the following criteria:

- Results of employee exposure monitoring, unless a negative exposure assessment has been made; and
- Observations, information, or calculations indicating employee exposure to asbestos, including any previous monitoring.

For *Class I* asbestos work, until employers document that employees will not be exposed in excess of the 8-hour TWA PEL and short-term exposure limit STEL, employers must assume that employee exposures are above those limits.

What is a negative exposure assessment?

For any specific asbestos job that trained employees perform, employers may show that exposures will be below the PELs (i.e., negative exposure assessment) through the following:

- Objective data demonstrating that ACM, or activities involving it, cannot release airborne fibers in excess of the 8-hour TWA PEL or STEL;
- Exposure data obtained within the past 12 months from prior monitoring of work operations closely resembling the employer's current work operations (the work operations that were previously monitored must have been conducted by employees whose training and experience were no more extensive than that of current employees, and the data must show a high degree of certainty that employee exposures will not exceed the 8-hour TWA PEL or STEL under current conditions); or
- Current initial exposure monitoring that used breathing zone air samples representing the 8-hour TWA and 30-minute short-term exposures for each employee in those operations most likely to result in exposures over the 8-hour TWA PEL for the entire asbestos job.

Are employers required to perform exposure monitoring?

Yes. Employers must determine employee exposure measurements from breathing zone air samples representing the 8-hour TWA and 30-minute short-term exposures for each employee.

Employers must take one or more samples representing full-shift exposure to determine the 8-hour TWA exposure in each work area. To determine short-term employee exposures, you must take one or more samples representing 30-minute exposures for the operations most likely to expose employees above the excursion limit in each work area.

You must also allow affected employees and their designated representatives to observe any employee exposure monitoring. When observation requires entry into a regulated area, you must provide and require the use of protective clothing and equipment.

When must employers conduct periodic monitoring?

For *Class I and II* jobs, employers must conduct monitoring daily that is representative of each employee working in a regulated area, unless you have produced a negative exposure assessment for the entire operation and nothing has changed. When all employees use supplied-air respirators operated in positive-pressure mode, however, you may discontinue daily monitoring. When employees perform *Class I* work using control methods not recommended in the standard, you must continue daily monitoring even when employees use supplied-air respirators.

For operations other than *Class I and II*, employers must monitor all work where exposures can possibly exceed the PEL often enough to validate the exposure prediction.

If periodic monitoring shows that certain employee exposures are below the 8-hour TWA PEL and the STEL, you may discontinue monitoring these employees' exposures.

Is additional monitoring ever needed?

Changes in processes, control equipment, personnel, or work practices that could result in new or additional exposures above the 8-hour TWA PEL or STEL require additional monitoring regardless of a previous negative exposure assessment for a specific job.

Are employers required to establish medical surveillance programs for employees?

It depends. Employers must provide a medical surveillance program for all employees who do the following:

- Engage in *Class I, II, or III* work or are exposed at or above the PEL or STEL for a combined total of 30 or more days per year; or
- Wear negative-pressure respirators.

In addition, a licensed physician must perform or supervise all medical exams and procedures that you provide at no cost to your employees and at a reasonable time.

Employers must make medical exams and consultations available to employees as follows:

- Prior to employee assignment to an area where negative pressure respirators are worn;
- Within 10 working days after the 30th day of combined engagement in Class I, II, and III work and exposure at or above a PEL, and at least annually thereafter; and
- When an examining physician suggests them more frequently.

If an employee was examined within the past 12 months and that exam meets the criteria of the standard, however, another medical exam is not required. Medical exams must include the following:

- Medical and work histories;
- Completion of a standardized questionnaire with the initial exam (see 29 CFR Part 1926.1101, Appendix D, Part 1) and an abbreviated standardized questionnaire with annual exams (see 29 CFR Part 1926.1101, Appendix D, Part 2);
- Physical exam focusing on the pulmonary and gastrointestinal systems; and
- Any other exams or tests deemed necessary by the examining physician.

Employers must provide the examining physician with the following:

- Copy of OSHA's asbestos standard and its appendices D, E, and I;
- Description of the affected employee's duties relating to exposure;
- Employee's representative exposure level or anticipated exposure level;

- Description of any personal protective equipment and respiratory equipment used; and
- Information from previous medical exams not otherwise available.

It is the employer's responsibility to obtain the physician's written opinion containing results of the medical exam as well as the following information:

- Any medical conditions of the employee that increase health risks from asbestos exposure.
- Any recommended limitations on the employee or protective equipment used.
- A statement that the employee has been informed of the results of the medical exam and any medical conditions resulting from asbestos exposure.
- A statement that the employee has been informed of the increased risk of lung cancer from the combined effect of smoking and asbestos exposure.

Note: A physician's written opinion must not reveal specific findings or diagnoses unrelated to occupational exposure to asbestos. You must provide a copy of the physician's written opinion to the employee involved within 30 days after receipt.

Do employers have to keep any employee records?

Yes. Employers must maintain employee records concerning objective data, exposure monitoring, and medical surveillance.

If using **objective data** to demonstrate that products made from or containing asbestos cannot release fibers in concentrations at or above the PEL or STEL, employers must keep an accurate record for as long as it is relied on and include the following information:

- Exempt products.
- Objective data source.
- Testing protocol, test results, and analysis of the material for release of asbestos.
- Exempt operation and support data descriptions.
- Relevant data for operations, materials, processes, or employee exposures.

Employers must keep records of all employee *exposure monitoring* for at least 30 years, including following information:

- Date of measurement.
- Operation involving asbestos exposure that you monitored.
- Methods of sampling and analysis that you used and evidence of their accuracy.
- Number, duration, and results of samples taken.
- Type of protective devices worn.
- Name, social security number, and exposures of the employees involved.

Employers must also make exposure records available when requested to affected employees, former employees, their designated representatives, and/or OSHA's Assistant Secretary.

In addition to retaining a copy of the information provided to the examining physician, employers must keep all *medical surveillance* records for the duration of an employee's employment plus 30 years, including the following information:

- Employee's name and social security number.
- Employee's medical exam results, including the medical history, questionnaires, responses, test results, and physician's recommendations.
- Physician's written opinions.
- Employee's medical complaints related to asbestos exposure.

Employers must also make employees' medical surveillance records available to them, as well as to anyone having specific written consent of an employee, and to OSHA's Assistant Secretary.

Also, employers must maintain other records. Employers must maintain all employee training records for 1 year beyond the last date of employment.

If data demonstrate ACM does not contain asbestos, building owners or employers must keep associated records for as long as they rely on them. Building owners must maintain written notifications on the identification, location, and quantity of any ACM or PACM for the duration of ownership, and transfer the records to successive owners.

When employers cease to do business without a successor to keep their records, employers must notify the Director of the National Institute for Occupational Safety and Health (NIOSH) at least 90 days prior to their disposal and transmit them as requested.

What is a regulated area?

A regulated area is a marked-off site where employees work with asbestos, including any adjoining areas where debris and waste from asbestos work accumulates or where airborne concentrations of asbestos exceed, or can possibly exceed, the PEL.

All *Class I, II, and III* asbestos work, or any other operations where airborne asbestos exceeds the PEL, must be performed within regulated areas. Only persons permitted by an employer and required by work duties to be present in regulated areas may enter a regulated area. The designated *competent person* supervises all asbestos work performed in this area.

Employers must mark off the regulated area in a manner that minimizes the number of persons within the area and protects persons outside the area from exposure to airborne asbestos. You may use critical barriers (i.e., plastic sheeting placed over all openings to the work area to prevent airborne asbestos from migrating to an adjacent area) or negative pressure enclosures to mark off a regulated area.

Posted warning signs demarcating the area must be easily readable and understandable. The signs must bear the following information:

DANGER

ASBESTOS

CANCER AND LUNG DISEASE HAZARD

AUTHORIZED PERSONNEL ONLY

RESPIRATORY AND PROTECTIVE CLOTHING

ARE REQUIRED IN THIS AREA

Employers must supply a respirator to all persons entering regulated areas. (See respiratory protection requirements elsewhere in this booklet.) Employees must not eat, drink, smoke, chew (tobacco or gum), or apply cosmetics in regulated areas.

An employer performing work in a regulated area must inform other employers onsite of the following:

- Nature of the work,
- Regulated area requirements, and
- Measures taken to protect onsite employees.

The contractor creating or controlling the source of asbestos contamination must abate the hazards. All employers with employees working near regulated areas must daily assess the enclosure's integrity or the effectiveness of control methods to prevent airborne asbestos from migrating.

General contractors on a construction project must oversee *all* asbestos work, even though they may not be the designated *competent person*. As supervisor of the entire project, the general contractor determines whether asbestos contractors comply with the standard and ensures that they correct any problems.

Who is responsible for communicating asbestos hazards at worksites?

The communication of asbestos hazards is vital to prevent further overexposure. Most asbestos-related construction involves previously installed building materials. Building/facility owners often are the only or best source of information concerning these materials.

Building/facility owners, as well as employers of workers who may be exposed to asbestos hazards, have specific duties under the standard.

Before work begins, building/facility owners must identify all thermal system insulation at the worksite, sprayed or troweled-on surfacing materials in buildings, and resilient flooring material installed before 1981. They also must notify the following persons of the presence, location, and quantity of ACM or PACM:

- Prospective employers applying or bidding for work in or adjacent to areas containing asbestos.
- Building owners' employees who work in or adjacent to these areas.
- Other employers on multi-employer worksites with employees working in or adjacent to these areas.
- All tenants who will occupy the areas containing ACM.

Employers discovering ACM on a worksite must notify the building/facility owner and other employers onsite within 24 hours regarding its presence, location, and quantity. You also must inform owners and employees working in nearby areas of the precautions taken to confine airborne asbestos. Within 10 days of project completion, you must inform building/facility owners and other employers onsite of the current locations and quantities of remaining ACM and any final monitoring results.

At any time, employers or building and facility owners may demonstrate that a PACM does not contain asbestos by inspecting the material in accordance with the requirements of the *Asbestos Hazard Emergency Response Act* (AHERA)

(40 CFR Part 763, Subpart E) or by performing tests of bulk samples collected in the manner described in 40 CFR Part 763.86. (See 29 CFR Part 1926.1101 for specific testing requirements.)

Employers do not have to inform employees of asbestos free building materials present; however, you must retain the information, data, and analysis supporting the determination. (See recordkeeping requirements elsewhere in this publication for more specific information.)

Does the OSHA standard require the posting of warning signs?

Yes. At the entrance to mechanical rooms or areas with ACM or PACM, the building/facility owner must post signs identifying the material present, its specific location, and appropriate work practices that ensure it is not disturbed.

Also, employers must post warning signs in regulated areas to inform employees of the dangers and necessary protective steps to take before entering. (See the regulated area requirements elsewhere in this publication.)

Must employers provide asbestos warning labels?

Employers must attach warning labels to all products and containers of asbestos, including waste containers, and all installed asbestos products, when possible. Labels must be printed in large, bold letters on a contrasting background and used in accordance with **OSHA's Hazard Communication Standard** (29 CFR Part1910.1200). All labels must contain a warning statement against breathing asbestos fibers and contain the following legend:

DANGER

CONTAINS ASBESTOS FIBERS

AVOID CREATING DUST

CANCER AND LUNG DISEASE HAZARD

Labels are not required if asbestos is present in concentrations less than 1 percent by weight. They also are not required if bonding agents, coatings, or binders have altered asbestos fibers, prohibiting the release of airborne asbestos over the PEL or STEL during reasonable use, handling, storage, disposal, processing, or transportation.

When building owners or employers identify previously installed asbestos or PACM, employers must attach or post clearly noticeable and readable labels or signs to inform employees which materials contain asbestos.

Do employers have to train employees regarding asbestos exposure?

Yes. Employers must provide a free training program for all employees who are likely to be exposed in excess of a PEL and for all employees performing *Class I* through *IV* asbestos operations. Employees must be trained prior to or at initial assignment and at least annually thereafter. Training courses must be easily understandable and include the following information:

- Ways to recognize asbestos.
- Adverse health effects of asbestos exposure.
- Relationship between smoking and asbestos in causing lung cancer.
- Operations that could result in asbestos exposure and the importance of protective controls to minimize exposure.
- Purpose, proper use, fitting instruction, and limitations of respirators.
- Appropriate work practices for performing asbestos jobs.
- Medical surveillance program requirements.
- Contents of the standard.
- Names, addresses, and phone numbers of public health organizations that provide information and materials or conduct smoking cessation programs.
- Sign and label requirements and the meaning of their legends.
- Written materials relating to employee training and selfhelp smoking cessation programs at no cost to employees.

Also, the following additional training requirements apply depending on the work class involved:

- For *Class I* operations and for *Class II* operations that require the use of critical barriers (or equivalent isolation methods) and/or negative pressure enclosures, training must be equivalent in curriculum, method, and length to the EPA Model Accreditation Plan (MAP) asbestos abatement worker training (see 40 CFR Part 763, Subpart E, Appendix C).
- For employees performing *Class II* operations involving one generic category of building materials containing asbestos (e.g., roofing, flooring, or

siding materials or transite panels), training may be covered in an 8-hour course that includes hands-on experience.

- For *Class III* operations, training must be equivalent in curriculum and method to the 16-hour *Operations and Maintenance* course developed by EPA for maintenance and custodial workers whose work disturbs ACM (see 40 CFR Part 763.92). The course must include hands-on training on proper respirator use and work practices.
- For *Class IV* operations, training must be equivalent in curriculum and method to EPA awareness training (see 29 CFR Part 1926.1101 for more information). Training must focus on the locations of ACM or PACM and the ways to recognize damage and deterioration and avoid exposure. The course must be at least 2 hours in length.

Note: Employers must provide OSHA's Assistant Secretary and the Director of NIOSH all information and training materials as requested.

Methods of Compliance

What methods must employers use to control asbestos exposure levels?

For all covered work, employers must use the following control methods to comply with the PEL and STEL:

Local exhaust ventilation equipped with HEPA-filter dust collection systems (a high-efficiency particulate air [HEPA] filter is capable of trapping and retaining at least 99.97 percent of all mono-dispersed particles of 0.3 micrometers in diameter).

- Enclosure or isolation of processes producing asbestos dust.
- Ventilation of the regulated area to move contaminated air away from the employees' breathing zone and toward a filtration or collection device equipped with a HEPA filter.
- Feasible engineering and work practice controls to reduce exposure to the lowest possible levels, supplemented by respirators to reach the PEL or STEL or lower.

Employers must use the following engineering controls and work practices for all operations regardless of exposure levels:

- Vacuum cleaners equipped with HEPA filters to collect all asbestos-containing or presumed asbestos-containing debris and dust.
- Wet methods or wetting agents to control employee exposures except when infeasible (e.g., due to the creation of electrical hazards, equipment malfunction, and slipping hazards).
- Prompt cleanup and disposal in leak-tight containers of asbestos-contaminated wastes and debris.

The following work practices and engineering controls are *prohibited* for all asbestos-related work or work that disturbs asbestos or PACM regardless of measured exposure levels or the results of initial exposure assessments:

- High-speed abrasive disc saws not equipped with a point-of-cut ventilator or enclosure with HEPA-filtered exhaust air.
- Compressed air to remove asbestos or ACM unless the compressed air is used with an enclosed ventilation system.
- Dry sweeping, shoveling, or other dry cleanup of dust and debris.
- Employee rotation to reduce exposure.

In addition, OSHA's asbestos standard has specific requirements for each class of asbestos work in construction.

What are the compliance requirements for Class I work?

A designated *competent person* must supervise all *Class I* work, including installing and operating the control system. The *competent person* must inspect onsite at least once during each work shift and upon employee request.

Employers must place critical barriers over all openings to regulated areas or use another barrier or isolation method to prevent airborne asbestos from migrating for the following jobs:

- All *Class I* jobs removing more than 25 linear or 10 square feet of thermal system insulation or surfacing material.
- All other *Class I* jobs without a negative exposure assessment.
- All jobs where employees are working in areas adjacent to a *Class I* regulated area.

If using other barriers or isolation methods instead of critical barriers, employers must perform perimeter area surveillance during each work shift. No asbestos dust should be visible. Perimeter monitoring must show that clearance levels are met (as contained in 40 CFR Part 763, Subpart E of the *EPA Asbestos in Schools* rule) or that perimeter area levels are no greater than background levels.

Employers must ensure the following for all *Class I* jobs:

- Isolating heating, ventilating, and air-conditioning (HVAC) systems in regulated areas by sealing with a double layer of 6 mil plastic or the equivalent.
- Placing impermeable drop cloths on surfaces beneath all removal activity.
- Covering and securing all objects within the regulated area with impermeable drop cloths or plastic sheeting.
- Ventilating the regulated area to move the contaminated air away from the employee breathing zone and toward a HEPA filtration or collection device for jobs without a negative exposure assessment or where exposure monitoring shows the PEL is exceeded.

In addition, employees performing *Class I* work must use one or more of the following control methods:

- Negative-pressure enclosure systems when the configuration of the work area does not make it infeasible to erect the enclosure.
- Glove bag systems to remove ACM or PACM from piping.
- Negative-pressure glove bag systems to remove asbestos or PACM from piping.
- Negative-pressure glove box systems to remove asbestos or ACM from pipe runs.
- Water spray process systems to remove asbestos or PACM from cold-line piping if employees carrying out the process have completed a 40-hour training course on its use in addition to training required for all employees performing *Class I* work.
- Small walk-in enclosure that accommodates no more than 2 people (mini-enclosure) if the disturbance or removal can be completely contained by the enclosure.

For the specifications, limitations, and recommended work practices of these required control methods, refer to *Occupational Exposure to Asbestos*, 29 CFR Part 1926.1101. Employers may use different or modified engineering and work practice controls if they adhere to the following provisions:

- Control method encloses, contains, or isolates the process or source of airborne asbestos dust, or captures and redirects the dust before it enters into the employees' breathing zone.

- Certified industrial hygienist or licensed professional engineer qualified as a project designer evaluates the work area, the projected work practices, and the engineering controls and certifies, in writing, that based on evaluations and data the planned control method adequately reduces direct and indirect employee exposure to or below the PEL under worst-case conditions. The planned control method also must prevent asbestos contamination outside the regulated area, as measured by sampling meeting the requirements of the *EPA Asbestos in Schools* rule or perimeter monitoring.
- Employer sends a copy of the evaluation and certification to the OSHA National Office, Office of Technical Support, Room N3653, 200 Constitution Avenue, N.W., Washington, DC 20210, before using alternative methods to remove more than 25 linear or 10 square feet of thermal system insulation or surfacing material.

What are the compliance requirements for Class II work?

In addition to all indoor *Class II* jobs without a negative exposure assessment, employers must use critical barriers over all openings to the regulated area or another barrier or isolation method to prevent airborne asbestos from migrating for the following:

- When changing conditions indicate exposure above the PEL, or
- When ACM is not removed substantially intact.

If using other barriers or isolation methods instead of critical barriers, employers must perform perimeter area monitoring to verify that the barrier works properly. In addition, impermeable drop cloths must cover all surfaces beneath removal activities.

All *Class II* asbestos work can use the same work practices and requirements as Class I asbestos jobs. Alternatively, *Class II* work can be performed using work practices set out in the standard for specific jobs.

For removing vinyl and asphalt flooring materials containing asbestos or installed in buildings constructed before 1981 and not verified as asbestos-free, employers must ensure that workers observe the following:

- Do not sand flooring or its backing,
- Do not rip up resilient sheeting,
- Do not dry sweep,
- Perform mechanical chipping only in a negative-pressure enclosure,

- Use vacuums equipped with HEPA filters to clean floors,
- Remove resilient sheeting by cutting with wetting of the snip point and wetting during delamination,
- Use wet methods to scrape residual adhesives and/or backing,
- Remove tiles intact, unless impossible (you may omit wetting when tiles are heated and removed intact), and
- Assume resilient flooring material—including associated mastic and backing—is asbestos-containing unless an industrial hygienist determines that it is asbestos-free.

To remove asbestos-containing roofing materials, employers must ensure that workers do the following:

- Remove them intact if feasible,
- Use wet methods when intact removal is infeasible, and
- Mist cutting machines continuously during use, unless the *competent person* determines misting to be unsafe.

When removing built-up roofs using a power roof cutter employers must ensure that workers observe the following procedures:

- Use power cutters equipped with HEPA dust collectors or perform HEPA vacuuming along the cut line for roofs that have asbestos-containing roofing felts and an aggregate surface.
- Use power cutters equipped with HEPA dust collectors, or perform HEPA vacuuming along the cut line, or gently sweep along the cut line and then carefully and completely wipe up the still-wet dust and debris that was acquired for roofs that have asbestos-containing roofing felts and a smooth surface.
- Do not drop or throw to the ground ACM that has been removed from a roof.
- Carry or pass the ACM to the ground by hand, or lower the material to the ground via covered, dust-tight chute, crane or hoist.
- Lower both intact ACM and non-intact ACM to the ground as soon as it is practicable, but no later than the end of the work shift.
- Keep material wet if it is not intact, or place it in impermeable waste bags, or wrap it in plastic sheeting while it remains on the roof.
- Lower to the ground, as soon as possible or by the end of the work shift, any unwrapped or unbagged roofing material using a covered, dust-tight chute, crane, or hoist.

- Place unwrapped materials in closed containers to prevent scattering dust after the materials reach the ground.
- Isolate roof level heating and ventilation air intake sources or shut down the ventilation system.

When removing cement-like asbestos-containing siding or shingles, or asbestos-containing transite panels on building exteriors other than roofs, employers must ensure that employees adhere to the following:

- Do not cut, abrade, or break siding, shingles, or transite panels unless methods less likely to result in asbestos fiber release cannot be used;
- Spray each panel or shingle with amended water before removing (amended water is water to which a surfactant [wetting agent] has been added to increase the ability of the liquid to penetrate ACM);
- Lower immediately to the ground any unwrapped or unbagged panels or shingles using a covered dust-tight chute, crane, or hoist, or place them in an impervious waste bag or wrap them in plastic heeting and lower them to the ground no later than the end of the work shift; and
- Cut nails with flat, sharp instruments.

When removing asbestos-containing gaskets, employers must ensure that employees do the following:

- Remove gaskets within glove bags if they are visibly deteriorated and unlikely to be removed intact;
- Wet the gaskets thoroughly with amended water prior to removing;
- Place the wet gaskets in a disposal container immediately; and
- Keep the residue wet if removed by scraping.

For removal of any other *Class II* ACM, employers must ensure that employees observe the following:

- Do not cut, abrade, or break the material unless infeasible;
- Wet the material thoroughly with amended water before and during removal;
- Remove the material intact, if possible; and
- Bag or wrap removed ACM immediately or keep it wet until transferred to a closed receptacle no later than the end of the work shift.

Employers may use different or modified engineering and work practice controls under the following conditions:

- If they can demonstrate that employee exposure will not exceed the PEL under any anticipated circumstances; and
- If a *competent person* evaluates the work area, the projected work practices, and the engineering controls and certifies, in writing, that these different or modified controls will reduce all employee exposure to or below the PELs under all expected conditions of use and that they meet the requirements of the standard. This evaluation must include, and be based on, data representing employee exposure during use of the controls under conditions closely resembling those of the current job. Also, the employees participating in the evaluation must not have better training and more experience than that of the employees who are to perform the current job.

What are the compliance requirements for Class III work?

Employers must use wet methods and local exhaust ventilation, to the extent feasible, during *Class III* work. When drilling, cutting, abrading, sanding, chipping, breaking, or sawing of asbestos-containing thermal system insulation or surfacing materials occurs, employers must use impermeable drop cloths as well as mini-enclosures, glove bag systems, or other effective isolation methods and ensure that workers wear respirators. If the material is not thermal system insulation or surfacing material and a negative exposure assessment has not been produced or monitoring shows the PEL is exceeded, employers must contain the area with impermeable drop cloths and plastic barriers or other isolation methods and ensure that employees wear respirators. (See also respirator requirements elsewhere in this publication.) In addition, the *competent person* must inspect often enough to assess changing conditions and upon employee request.

What are the compliance requirements for Class IV work?

Employees conducting Class IV asbestos work must have attended an asbestos awareness training program. They must use wet methods and HEPA vacuums to promptly clean asbestos-containing or presumed asbestos-containing debris. When cleaning debris and waste in regulated areas, employees must wear respirators. In areas where thermal system insulation or surfacing material is present, workers must assume that all waste and debris contain asbestos.

Does the *competent person* have duties that apply to more than one work class?

Yes. For *Class II, III, and IV* jobs, the *competent person* must inspect often enough to assess changing conditions and upon employee request.

For *Class I or II* asbestos work, the *competent person* must ensure the integrity of the enclosures or other containments by onsite inspection and supervise the following activities:

- Setup of regulated areas, enclosures, or other containments.
- Setup procedures to control entry to and exit from the enclosure or area.
- Employee exposure monitoring by ensuring it is properly conducted.
- Use of required protective clothing and equipment by employees working within the enclosure or using glove bags (a plastic bag-like enclosure affixed around ACM, with glove-like appendages through which materials and tools may be handled).
- Setup, removal, and performance of engineering controls, work practices, and personal protective equipment through onsite inspection.
- Use of hygiene facilities by employees.
- Required decontamination procedures.
- Notification requirements.

What does the OSHA standard require concerning respirators?

Employees must use respirators during the following activities:

- *Class I* asbestos jobs.
- *Class II* work where ACM is not removed substantially intact.
- *Class II and III* work not using wet methods.
- *Class II and III* work without a negative exposure assessment.
- *Class III* jobs where thermal system insulation or surfacing ACM or PACM is cut, abraded, or broken.
- *Class IV* work within a regulated area where respirators are required.
- Work where employees are exposed above the TWA or excursion limit.
- Emergencies.

Employers must provide respirators at no cost to workers, selecting the appropriate type from among those certified by NIOSH.

Employers must provide employees performing *Class I* work with full-facepiece supplied air respirators operated in pressure-demand mode and equipped with an auxiliary positive-pressure, self-contained breathing apparatus when exposure levels exceed 1 f/cc as an 8-hour TWA.

Employers must provide half-mask purifying respirators—other than disposable respirators—equipped with high efficiency filters for *Class II and III* asbestos jobs where work disturbs thermal system insulation or surfacing ACM or PACM.

If a particular job is not *Class I, II, or III* and exposures are above the PEL or STEL, the asbestos standard, 29 CFR Part 1926.1101, contains a table specifying types of respirators to use.

According to 29 CFR Part 1910.134, employers must institute a respiratory program that includes the following:

- Procedures for selecting respirators for use in the workplace;
- Fit testing procedures for tight-fitting respirators;
- Procedures for proper use of respirators in routine and reasonably foreseeable emergency situations;
- Procedures and schedules for cleaning, disinfecting, storing, inspecting, repairing, discarding, and maintaining respirators;
- Procedures to ensure adequate air quality, quantity, and flow of breathing air for atmosphere-supplying respirators;
- Training of employees in the respiratory hazards to which they are potentially exposed during routine and emergency situations;
- Training of employees in the proper use and maintenance of respirators, including putting on and removing them, and any limitations on their use; and
- Procedures for regularly evaluating the effectiveness of the program.

(See Respiratory Protection, 29 CFR Part 1910.134, for complete program requirements.)

With regard to fit testing, employers must do the following:

- Ensure that employees are fit tested with the same make, model, style, and size of respirator that they will be using;
- Ensure that employees using a tight-fitting facepiece respirator pass an appropriate qualitative fit test (QLFT) or quantitative fit test (QNFT);
- Ensure that an employee using a tight-fitting facepiece respirator is fit tested prior to initial use of the respirator, whenever a different size, style,

model or make of respirator facepiece is used, and at least annually thereafter.

- Conduct an additional fit test whenever an employee reports (or the employer, physician or other licensed health-care professional, supervisor, or program administrator makes) visual observations of changes in an employee's physical condition that could affect respirator fit. Such conditions include, but are not limited to, facial scarring, dental changes, cosmetic surgery, or an obvious change in body weight.

Employers must not assign any employee to tasks requiring respirator use who, based on the most recent physical exam and the examining physician's recommendations, would be unable to function normally. Employers must assign such employees to other jobs or give them the opportunity to transfer to different positions in the same geographical area and with the same seniority, status, pay rate, and job benefits as they had before transferring, if such positions are available.

Do employers have to provide protective clothing for employees?

Employers must provide and require the use of protective clothing—such as coveralls or similar whole-body clothing, head coverings, gloves, and foot coverings—for the following:

- Employees exposed to airborne asbestos exceeding the PEL or STEL;
- Work without a negative exposure assessment; or
- Employees performing *Class I* work involving the removal of over 25 linear or 10 square feet of thermal system insulation or surfacing ACM or PACM.

Employers must ensure that the laundering of contaminated clothing does not release airborne asbestos in excess of the PEL or STEL. Employers who give contaminated clothing to other persons for laundering must inform them of the requirement to follow procedures that do not release airborne asbestos in excess of the PEL or STEL.

Employers must transport contaminated clothing in sealed, impermeable bags or other closed impermeable containers bearing appropriate labels. (See the hazard communication section elsewhere in this publication for label requirements.)

The *competent person* must examine employee worksuits at least once per work shift for rips or tears. Rips or tears found while an employee is working must be mended or the worksuit replaced immediately.

What are the hygiene-related requirements for employees performing Class I asbestos work involving more than 25 linear feet or 10 square feet of thermal system insulation or surfacing ACM or PACM?

For this class of asbestos work, the requirements are as follows:

- Employers must create a decontamination area adjacent to and connected with the regulated area.
- Workers must enter and exit the regulated area through the decontamination area.

The decontamination area must include an equipment room, shower area, and clean room in series and comply with the following:

- Equipment room must have impermeable, labeled bags and containers to store and dispose of contaminated protective equipment.
- Shower area must be adjacent to both the equipment and clean rooms, unless work is performed outdoors or this arrangement is not feasible (in either case, employers must ensure that employees remove asbestos contamination from their worksuits in the equipment room using a HEPA vacuum before proceeding to a shower not adjacent to the work area or remove their contaminated worksuits in the equipment room, don clean worksuits, and proceed to a shower not adjacent to the work area).
- Clean room must have a locker or appropriate storage container for each employee.

Note: When it is not feasible to provide a change area adjacent to the work area, or when the work is performed outdoors, employees may clean protective clothing with a portable HEPA vacuum before leaving the regulated area. Employees then must shower and change into "street clothing" in a clean change area meeting the requirements described above.

To enter the regulated area, employees must pass through the equipment room. But before entering the regulated area, employees must do the following:

- Enter the decontamination area through the clean room.
- Remove and deposit street clothing within a provided locker.
- Put on protective clothing and respiratory protection before leaving the clean area.

Before exiting the regulated area, employees must do the following:

- Remove all gross contamination and debris.
- Remove protective clothing in the equipment room (depositing the clothing in labeled, impermeable bags or containers).
- Remove respirators in the shower and then shower before entering the clean room to change into "street clothing."

Note: When workers consume food or beverages at the *Class I* worksite, employers must provide lunch areas with airborne asbestos levels below the PEL and/or excursion limit.

What are the hygiene-related requirements for employees performing other Class I asbestos work and Class II and III asbestos work where exposures exceed a PEL or where a negative exposure assessment has not been produced?

For this class of asbestos work, the requirements are as follows:

- Employers must establish an equipment room or area adjacent to the regulated area for the decontamination of employees and their equipment.
- Workers must cover area with an impermeable drop cloth on the floor or horizontal work surface and must be large enough to accommodate equipment cleaning and personal protective equipment removal without spreading contamination beyond the area.
- Workers must clean area with a HEPA vacuum before removing work clothing.
- Workers must clean all equipment and surfaces of containers filled with ACM before removal.
- Employers must ensure employees enter and exit the regulated area through the equipment room or area.

What are the hygiene-related requirements for employees performing Class IV work?

For this class of asbestos work, the requirements are as follows:

- Employers must ensure that workers cleaning up dust, waste, and debris while a *Class I, II, or III* activity is still in progress observe the hygiene practices required of the workers performing that activity.

- Workers cleaning up asbestos-containing surfacing material or thermal system insulation debris from a *Class I or III* activity after the activity is finished must be provided decontamination facilities required for *Class I* work involving less than 25 linear or 10 square feet of material, or for *Class III* work where exposure exceeds a PEL or no negative exposure assessment exists.

Note: For *any* class of asbestos work, employers must ensure that workers do not smoke in any work area with asbestos exposure.

What are an employer's housekeeping responsibilities?

Asbestos waste, scrap, debris, bags, containers, equipment, and contaminated clothing consigned for disposal must be collected and disposed of in sealed, labeled, impermeable bags or other closed, labeled impermeable containers. When vacuuming methods are selected, employees must use and empty HEPA-filtered vacuuming equipment carefully and in a way that will minimize asbestos reentry into the workplace.

Unless the building/facility owner demonstrates that the flooring does not contain asbestos, all vinyl and asphalt flooring material must be maintained in accordance with the following conditions:

- Sanding flooring material is prohibited.
- Employees stripping finishes must use wet methods and low abrasion pads at speeds lower than 300 revolutions per minute.
- Burnishing or dry buffing may be done only on flooring with enough finish that the pad cannot contact the flooring material.
- Employees must not dust, dry sweep, or vacuum without a HEPA filter in an area containing thermal system insulation or surfacing material or visibly deteriorated ACM.
- Employees must promptly clean up the waste and debris and accompanying dust, and dispose of it in leak-tight, labeled containers.

For a quick reference to the OSHA standard's provisions by work class, please see the following table.

Quick Reference of Provisions by Work Class*

	Class I	Class II	Class III	Class IV
Definition	Removal of thermal system insulation (TSI) and surfacing material (SM) containing > 1% asbestos	Removal of material other than TSI or SM containing > 1% asbestos	Maintenance and repair operations disturbing material containing > 1% asbestos	Housekeeping and custodial cleanup of dust, waste, and debris from Class I, II, or III activities
Regulated Areas	Required (warning signs mandatory)	Required (warning signs mandatory)	Required (warning signs mandatory)	Required (warning signs mandatory)
competent person	•Must be onsite •Must inspect each workshift •Must attend supervisory training	•Must be onsite •Must inspect often •Must attend supervisory training	•Must be onsite •Must inspect often •Must attend operational and maintenance training	•Must be onsite •Must inspect often •Must attend operational and maintenance training
Air Monitoring	•Initial if no negative exposure assessment (NEA) •Daily unless positive pressure mode respirator is used •Additional if conditions change **Note:** Terminate if < permissible exposure limits (PELs)	•Initial if no NEA •Daily unless positive pressure mode respirator is used •Additional if conditions change **Note:** Terminate if < PELs	•Initial if no NEA •Periodic to accurately predict if > PELs •Additional if conditions change **Note:** Terminate if < PELs	•Initial if no NEA •Periodic to accurately predict if > PELs •Additional if conditions change **Note:** Terminate if < PELs
Medical > Surveillance	Required if Wearing negative- pressure respirator, or > 30 days of work/year	Required if •Wearing negative-pressure respirator, or •> 30 days of work/year	Required if Wearing negative-pressure respirator, or > 30 days of work/year	Required if •Wearing negative-pressure respirator, or •> PEL for more than 30 days/year
Respirators	Mandatory for all Class I jobs	Mandatory if •Non-intact removal, or •No NEA, or •> PEL, or •Dry removal (except for roofing), or •In emergencies	Mandatory if •No NEA, or •TSI or SM disturbed, or •> PEL, or •Dry removal (except for roofing), or •In emergencies	Mandatory •In regulated area where required, or •If > PEL, or •In emergencies
Protective Clothing and Equipment	Required for all jobs if •> 25 linear or 10 square feet of TSI or •SM removal, or •No NEA, or •> PEL	Required for all jobs if •No NEA, or •> PEL	Required for all jobs if •No NEA, or •> PEL	Required for all jobs if •No NEA, or •> PEL

*This is an overview of the standards' requirements. You must consult the standard for the specifics of the requirements for each class.

	Class I	Class II	Class III	Class IV
Training	Equivalent to EPA Model Accreditation Plan (MAP) asbestos abatement workers course	Equivalent to MAP course if critical barriers required; otherwise, train on specific work practices and engineering controls that must be used	Equivalent to AHERA course for maintenance and custodial staff	Equivalent to AHERA course for maintenance and custodial staff
Employee and Equipment Decontamination	Required if > 25 linear or 10 square feet TSI or SM removal •Full decon unit •Equipment room, shower, and clean room in series connected to the regulated area; other decon facility arrangements are acceptable if the specified series arrangement is not feasible (see 29 CFR Part 1926.1101, Subpart Z) •Lunch areas **Note:** Must follow detailed decontamination procedures (see 29 CFR Part 1926.1101(j)(1)(iii) If < 25 linear or 10 square feet TSI or SM removal •Equipment room/area required •Impermeable dropcloths required •Area must accommodate cleanup •Must decontaminate all personal protective equipment (PPE) •Must enter regulated area through equipment room/decon area No smoking in work area	If > PEL or no NEA Equipment room/area required Impermeable dropcloths required Area must accommodate cleanup Must clean work clothes with HEPA vacuum before removal Must Decontaminate all PPE Must enter regulated area through equipment room/decon area Must enter regulated area through equipment room/decon area No smoking in work area	> PEL or no NEA Equipment room/area required Impermeable dropcloths required Area must accommodate cleanup Must clean work clothes with HEPA vacuum before removal Must Decontaminate all PPE Must enter regulated area through equipment room/decon area Must enter regulated area through equipment room/decon area NEA must vacuum No smoking in work area	If cleaning up asbestos containing surfacing material or thermal system insulation debris from a Class I or III activity after the activity is finished •Equipment room/area required •Dropcloths required •Area must accommodate cleanup •Must clean work clothes with HEPA vacuum before removal •Must decontaminate all PPE •Must enter regulated area through equipment room/decon area No smoking in work area **Note:** If cleaning up dust, waste, and debris while a Class I, II, or III activity is still in progress, the requirements of that activity apply.
Generally Required Work Practices and Engineering Controls	•Wet methods •HEPA vacuum •Prompt cleanup/disposal	•Wet methods •HEPA vacuum •Prompt cleanup/disposal	•Wet methods •HEPA vacuum •Prompt cleanup/disposal	•Wet methods •HEPA vacuum •Prompt cleanup/disposal
Required Work Practices and Engineering Controls to Comply with PELs	•HEPA local exhaust •Enclosure or isolation •Directed ventilation •Other work practices •Respirators	•HEPA local exhaust •Enclosure •Directed ventilation •Other work practices •Respirators	•HEPA local exhaust •Enclosure •Directed ventilation •Other work practices •Respirators	•HEPA local exhaust •Enclosure •Directed ventilation •Other work practices •Respirators
Prohibited Work Practices and Administrative Controls	•High-speed abrasive disc saws without HEPA •Compressed air without capture device •Dry sweeping/shoveling	•High-speed abrasive disc saws without HEPA •Compressed air without capture device •Dry sweeping/shoveling	•High-speed abrasive disc saws without HEPA •Compressed air without capture device •Dry sweeping/shoveling	•High-speed abrasive disc saws without HEPA •Compressed air without capture device •Employee rotation

	Class I	Class II	Class III	Class IV
Controls and Work Practices	•Critical barriers/isolation methods required if • > 25 linear or 10 square feet of TSI or SM removal • < 25 linear or 10 square feet of TSI or SM removal only if no NEA or there are adjacent workers •HVAC isolation required •Impermeable dropcloths required •Directed ventilation required if no NEA or > a PEL •Objects must be covered One or more of the following controls must be used: •Negative-pressure enclosure •Glove bag •Negative-pressure glove bag •Negative pressure glove box •Water spray process •Mini enclosure	For indoor work only •Critical barriers/isolation methods required if • no NEA • likely > a PEL • non-intact removal •Impermeable dropcloths required For removal of vinyl and asphalt flooring materials •No sanding •HEPA vacuum •Wet methods •No dry sweeping •Any mechanical chipping must be done in negative-pressure enclosure •Intact removal if possible •Dry heat removal allowed •Assume contains asbestos without an analysis For removal of roofing materials •Intact removal if possible •Wet methods if feasible •Cutting machine misting •HEPA-vacuum debris •Lower to ground as soon as possible but no later than day's end •Control dust of unbagged material •Prevent intake of airborne asbestos< through roof vent system Class II For removal of cement-like siding, shingles, or transite panels •Intact removal if possible •Wet Methods •Lower to ground via dust-tight chute, crane, or hoist immediately or place in an impervious waste bag or wrap in plastic sheeting and lower to ground by day's end •Cut nail heads For removal of gaskets •Use glove bags if not intact •Wet removal •Prompt disposal •Wet scraping Additional requirements •Wet methods •Intact removal if possible •Cutting, abrading, or breaking prohibited	•Critical barriers required • If no NEA • > Pel via monitoring •Impermeable dropcloths required •Local HEPA exhaust required **Note:** Enclosure or isolation of operation required if TSI or SM is drilled, cut, abraded, sanded, sawed, or chipped	See Generally Required Work Practices and Engineering Controls in this table

OSHA Assistance

OSHA can provide extensive help through a variety of programs, including technical assistance about effective safety and health programs, state plans, workplace consultations, voluntary protection programs, strategic partnerships, and training and education, and more. An overall commitment to workplace safety and health can add value to your business, to your workplace, and to your life.

What are safety and health system management guidelines?

Effective management of worker safety and health protection is a decisive factor in reducing the extent and severity of work-related injuries and illnesses and their related costs. In fact, an effective safety and health program forms the basis of good worker protection and can save time and money—about $4 for every dollar spent—and increase productivity and reduce worker injuries, illnesses, and related worker compensation costs.

To assist employers and employees in developing effective safety and health programs, OSHA published recommended *Safety and Health Program Management Guidelines* (*Federal Register* 54(16): 3904-3916, January 26, 1989). These voluntary guidelines can be applied to all places of employment covered by OSHA.

The guidelines identify four general elements critical to the development of a successful safety and health management system:

- Management leadership and employee involvement,
- Worksite analysis,
- Hazard prevention and control, and
- Safety and health training.

The guidelines recommend specific actions, under each of these general elements, to achieve an effective safety and health program. The *Federal Register* notice is available online at www.osha.gov.

What are state programs?

The *Occupational Safety and Health Act of 1970* (OSH Act) encourages states to develop and operate their own job safety and health plans. OSHA approves and monitors these plans. There are currently 26 state plans: 23 cover both private and public (state and local government) employment; 3 states, Connecticut, New Jersey, and New York, cover the public sector only. States and territories with their own OSHA-approved occupational safety and health plans must adopt standards identical to, or at least as effective as, the federal standards.

How do I obtain consultation services?

Consultation assistance is available on request to employers who want help in establishing and maintaining a safe and healthful workplace. Largely funded by OSHA, the service is provided at no cost to the employer. Primarily developed for smaller employers with more hazardous operations, the consultation service is delivered by state governments employing professional safety and health consultants. Comprehensive assistance includes an appraisal of all mechanical systems, work practices, and occupational safety and health hazards of the workplace and all aspects of the employer's present job safety and health program. In addition, the service offers assistance to employers in developing and implementing an effective safety and health program. No penalties are proposed or citations issued for hazards identified by the consultant. OSHA provides consultation assistance to the employer with the assurance that his or her name and firm and any information about the workplace will not be routinely reported to OSHA enforcement staff.

Under the consultation program, certain exemplary employers may request participation in OSHA's Safety and Health Achievement Recognition Program (SHARP). Eligibility for participation in SHARP includes receiving a comprehensive consultation visit, demonstrating exemplary achievements in workplace safety and health by abating all identified hazards, and developing an excellent safety and health program.

Employers accepted into SHARP may receive an exemption from programmed inspections (not complaint or accident investigation inspections) for a period of 1 year. For more information concerning consultation assistance, see the list of consultation projects listed at the end of this publication.

What are Voluntary Protection Programs (VPPs)?

Voluntary Protection Programs and onsite consultation services, when coupled with an effective enforcement program, expand worker protection to help meet the goals of the OSH Act. The three VPPs—Star, Merit, and Demonstration—

are designed to recognize outstanding achievements by companies that have successfully incorporated comprehensive safety and health programs into their total management system. The VPPs motivate others to achieve excellent safety and health results in the same outstanding way as they establish a cooperative relationship between employers, employees, and OSHA.

For additional information on VPPs and how to apply, contact the OSHA regional offices listed at the end of this publication.

What is the Strategic Partnership Program?

OSHA's Strategic Partnership Program, the newest member of OSHA's cooperative programs, helps encourage, assist, and recognize the efforts of partners to eliminate serious workplace hazards and achieve a high level of worker safety and health. Whereas OSHA's Consultation Program and VPP entail one-on-one relationships between OSHA and individual worksites, most strategic partnerships seek to have a broader impact by building cooperative relationships with groups of employers and employees. These partnerships are voluntary, cooperative relationships between OSHA, employers, employee representatives, and others (e.g., trade unions, trade and professional associations, universities, and other government agencies).

For more information on this program, contact your nearest OSHA office, or visit OSHA's website at www.osha.gov.

Does OSHA offer training and education?

OSHA's area offices offer a variety of information services, such as compliance assistance, technical advice, publications, audiovisual aids and speakers for special engagements. OSHA's Training Institute in Des Plaines, IL, provides basic and advanced courses in safety and health for federal and state compliance officers, state consultants, federal agency personnel, and private sector employers, employees, and their representatives.

The OSHA Training Institute also has established OSHA Training Institute Education Centers to address the increased demand for its courses from the private sector and from other federal agencies. These centers are nonprofit colleges universities, and other organizations that have been selected after a competition for participation in the program. OSHA also provides funds to nonprofit organizations, through grants, to conduct workplace training and education in subjects where OSHA believes there is a lack of workplace training. Grants are awarded annually. Grant recipients are expected to contribute 20 percent of the total grant cost. For more information on grants, training, and education, contact the OSHA Training Institute, Office of Training and Education, 1555 Times Drive, Des Plaines, IL 60018, (847) 297-4810. For further information on any OSHA program, contact your nearest OSHA area or regional office listed at the end of this publication.

Does OSHA provide any information electronically?

OSHA has a variety of materials and tools available on its website—www.osha.gov. These include e-Tools such as Expert Advisors, Electronic Compliance Assistance Tools (e-CATs), Technical Links; regulations, directives, publications; videos, and other information for employers and employees. OSHA's software programs and compliance assistance tools walk you through challenging safety and health issues and common problems to find the best solutions for your workplace.

OSHA's CD-ROM includes standards, interpretations, directives, and more and can be purchased on CD-ROM from the U.S. Government Printing Office. To order, write to the Superintendent of Documents, P.O. Box 371954, Pittsburgh, PA 15250-7954 or phone (202) 512-1800.

How do I learn more about related OSHA publications?

OSHA has an extensive publications program. For a listing of free or sales items, visit OSHA's website at www.osha.gov or contact the OSHA Publications Office, U.S. Department of Labor, 200 Constitution Avenue, N.W., N-3101, Washington, DC 20210. Telephone (202) 693-1888 or fax to (202) 693-2498.

How do I contact OSHA about emergencies, complaints, or further assistance?

To report an emergency, file a complaint, or seek OSHA advice, assistance, or products, call 1-800-321-OSHA or contact your nearest OSHA regional or area office listed at the end of this publication. The teletypewriter (TTY) number is 1-877-889-5627.

You can also file a complaint online and obtain more information on OSHA federal and state programs by visiting OSHA's website at www.osha.gov.

For more information on grants, training, and education, contact the OSHA Training Institute, Office of Training and Education, 1555 Times Drive, Des Plaines, IL 60018, (847) 297-4810, or see **Outreach** on OSHA's website at www.osha.gov.

OSHA Office Directory

OSHA Regional Offices

Region I
(CT,* ME, MA, NH, RI, VT*)
JFK Federal Building, Room E340
Boston, MA 02203
(617) 565-9860

Region II
(NJ,* NY,* PR,* VI*)
201 Varick Street, Room 670
New York, NY 10014
(212) 337-2378

Region III
(DE, DC, MD,* PA,* VA,* WV)
The Curtis Center
170 S. Independence Mall West
Suite 740 West
Philadelphia, PA 19106-3309
(215) 861-4900

Region IV
(AL, FL, GA, KY,* MS, NC,* SC,* TN*)
SNAF
61 Forsyth Street SW, Room 6T50
Atlanta, GA 30303
(404) 562-2300

Region V
(IL, IN,* MI,* MN,* OH, WI)
230 South Dearborn Street,
Room 3244
Chicago, IL 60604
(312) 353-2220

Region VI
(AR, LA, NM,* OK, TX)
525 Griffin Street, Room 602
Dallas, TX 75202
(214) 767-4731 or 4736 x224

Region VII
(IA,* KS, MO, NE)
City Center Square
1100 Main Street, Suite 800
Kansas City, MO 64105
(816) 426-5861

Region VIII
(CO, MT, ND, SD, UT,* WY*)
1999 Broadway, Suite 1690
PO Box 46550
Denver, CO 80202-5716
(303) 844-1600

Region IX
(American Samoa, AZ,* CA,* HI, NV,* Northern Mariana Islands)
71 Stevenson Street, Room 420
San Francisco, CA 94105
(415) 975-4310

Region X
(AK,* ID, OR,* WA*)
1111 Third Avenue, Suite 715
Seattle, WA 98101-3212
(206) 553-5930

*These states and territories operate their own OSHA-approved job safety and health programs (Connecticut, New Jersey, and New York plans cover public employees only). States with approved programs must have a standard that is identical to, or at least as effective as, the federal standard.

OSHA Area Offices

Anchorage, AK
(907) 271-5152

Birmingham, AL
(205) 731-1534

Mobile, AL
(251) 441-6131

Little Rock, AR
(501) 324-6291(5818)

Phoenix, AZ
(602) 640-2348

Sacramento, CA
(916) 566-7471

San Diego, CA
(619) 557-5909

Denver, CO
(303) 844-5285

Greenwood Village, CO
(303) 843-4500

Bridgeport, CT
(203) 579-5581

Hartford, CT
(860) 240-3152

Wilmington, DE
(302) 573-6518

Fort Lauderdale, FL
(954) 424-0242

Jacksonville, FL
(904) 232-2895

Tampa, FL
(813) 626-1177

Savannah, GA
(912) 652-4393

Smyrna, GA
(770) 984-8700

Tucker, GA
(770) 493-6644/6742/8419

Des Moines, IA
(515) 284-4794

Boise, ID
(208) 321-2960

Calumet City, IL
(708) 891-3800

Des Plaines, IL
(847) 803-4800

Fairview Heights, IL
(618) 632-8612

North Aurora, IL
(630) 896-8700

Peoria, IL
(309) 671-7033

Indianapolis, IN
(317) 226-7290

Wichita, KS
(316) 269-6644

Frankfort, KY
(502) 227-7024

Baton Rouge, LA
(225) 389-0474 (0431)

Braintree, MA
(617) 565-6924

Methuen, MA
(617) 565-8110

Springfield, MA
(413) 785-0123

Linthicum, MD
(410) 865-2055/2056

Augusta, ME
(207) 622-8417

Bangor, ME
(207) 941-8177

Portland, ME
(207) 780-3178

Lansing, MI
(517) 327-0904

Minneapolis, MN
(612) 664- 5460

Kansas City, MO
(816) 483-9531

St. Louis, MO
(314) 425-4249

Jackson, MS
(601) 965-4606

Billings, MT
(406) 247-7494

Raleigh, NC
(919) 856-4770

Bismark, ND
(701) 250-4521

Omaha, NE
(402) 221-3182

Concord, NH
(603) 225-1629

Avenel, NJ
(732) 750-3270

Hasbrouck Heights, NJ
(201) 288-1700

Marlton, NJ
(856) 757-5181

Parsippany, NJ
(973) 263-1003

Carson City, NV
(775) 885-6963

Albany, NY
(518) 464-4338

Bayside, NY
(718) 279-9060

Bowmansville, NY
(716) 684-3891

New York, NY
(212) 337-2636

North Syracuse, NY
(315) 451-0808

Tarrytown, NY
(914) 524-7510

Westbury, NY
(516) 334-3344

Cincinnati, OH
(513) 841-4132

Cleveland, OH
(216) 522-3818

Columbus, OH
(614) 469-5582

Toledo, OH
(419) 259-7542

Oklahoma City, OK
(405) 278-9560

Portland, OR
(503) 326-2251

Allentown, PA
(610) 776-0592

Erie, PA
(814) 833-5758

Harrisburg, PA
(717) 782-3902

Philadelphia, PA
(215) 597-4955

Pittsburgh, PA
(412) 395-4903

Wilkes-Barre, PA
(570) 826-6538

Guaynabo, PR
(787) 277-1560

Providence, RI
(401) 528-4669

Columbia, SC
(803) 765-5904

Nashville, TN
(615) 781-5423

Austin, TX
(512) 916-5783 (5788)

Corpus Christi, TX
(361) 888-3420

Dallas, TX
(214) 320-2400 (2558)

El Paso, TX
(915) 534-6251

Fort Worth, TX
(817) 428-2470 (485-7647)

Houston, TX
(281) 591-2438 (2787)

Houston, TX
(281) 286-0583/0584 (5922)

Lubbock, TX
(806) 472-7681 (7685)

Salt Lake City, UT
(801) 530-6901

Norfolk, VA
(757) 441-3820

Bellevue, WA
(206) 553-7520

Appleton, WI
(920) 734-4521

Eau Claire, WI
(715) 832-9019

Madison, WI
(608) 264-5388

Milwaukee, WI
(414) 297-3315

Charleston, WV
(304) 347-5937

OSHA-Approved State Plans

Commissioner
Alaska Department of Labor
1111 W. 8th Street, Room 308
P.O. Box 21149
Juneau, AK 99802-1149
(907) 465-2700

Director
Industrial Commission of Arizona
800 W. Washington
Phoenix, AZ 85007
(602) 542-5795

Director
California Department of Industrial Relations
455 Golden Gate Avenue
10th Floor
San Francisco, CA 94102
(415) 703-5050

Commissioner
Connecticut Department of Labor
200 Folly Brook Boulevard
Wethersfield, CT 06109
(860) 263-6505

Director
Hawaii Department of Labor and Industrial Relations
830 Punchbowl Street
Honolulu, HI 96831
(808) 586-8844

Commissioner
Iowa Division of Labor
1000 E. Grand Avenue
Des Moines, IA 50319
(515) 281-3447

Commissioner
Indiana Department of Labor
State Office Building
402 West Washington Street
Room W195
Indianapolis, IN 46204
(317) 232-2378

Secretary
Kentucky Labor Cabinet
1047 U.S. Highway 127 South Suite 4
Frankfort, KY 40601
(502) 564-3070

Commissioner
Maryland Division of Labor and Industry
Department of Labor Licensing and Regulation
MOSH
1100 N. Eutaw Street, Room 613
Baltimore, MD 21201-2206
(410) 767-2215

Director
Michigan Department of Consumer and Industry Services
P.O. Box 30643
7150 Harris Drive
Lansing, MI 48909
(517) 373-7230

Commissioner
Minnesota Department of Labor and Industry
443 Lafayette Road
St. Paul, MN 55155
(651) 284-5010

Commissioner
North Carolina Department of Labor
4 West Edenton Street
Raleigh, NC 27601-1092
(919) 807-2900

Commissioner
New Jersey Department of Labor
John Fitch Plaza — Labor Building
Market and Warren Streets
P.O. Box 110
Trenton, NJ 08625-0110
(609) 292-2975

Secretary
New Mexico Environment Department
1190 St. Francis Drive
P.O. Box 26110
Santa Fe, NM 87502
(505) 827-2850

Commissioner
New York Department of Labor
W. Averell Harriman State Office
Building-12, Room 500
Albany, NY 12240
(518) 457-2741

Administrator
Nevada Division of Industrial Relations
400 West King Street, Suite 400
Carson City, NV 89703
(775) 684-7260

Administrator
Oregon Department of Consumer and Business Services
Occupational Safety and Health Division (OR-OSHA)
350 Winter Street, N.E. Room 430
Salem, OR 97310-3882
(503) 378-3272

Secretary
Puerto Rico Department of Labor and Human Resources
Prudencio Rivera Martinez Building
505 Munoz Rivera Avenue
Hato Rey, PR 00918
(787) 754-2119

Director
South Carolina Department of Labor
Licensing and Regulation
Koger Office Park
Kingstree Building
110 Centerview Drive
P.O. Box 11329
Columbia, SC 29211
(803) 896-4300

Commissioner
Tennessee Department of Labor and Workforce Development
710 James Robertson Parkway
Andrew Johnson Tower
Nashville, TN 37243-0659
(615) 741-2582

Commissioner
Labor Commission of Utah
160 East 300 South Street
3rd Floor
P.O. Box 146650
Salt Lake City, UT 84111
(801) 530-6901

Commissioner
Virginia Department of Labor and Industry
Powers-Taylor Building
13 South 13th Street
Richmond, VA 23219
(804) 786-2377

Commissioner
Virgin Islands Department of Labor
2203 Church Street
Christiansted
St. Croix, VI 00820-4660
(340) 773-1990

Commissioner
Vermont Department of Labor and Industry
National Life Building—Drawer 20
120 State Street
Montpelier, VT 05620-3401
(802) 828-2288

Director
Washington Department of Labor and Industries
P.O. Box 44001
Olympia, WA 98504-4001
(360) 902-4200
(360) 902-5430

Administrator
Worker's Safety and
Compensation Division (WSC)
Wyoming Department of Employment
Herschler Building, 2nd Floor East
122 West 25th Street
Cheyenne, WY 82002
(307) 777-7786

OSHA Consultation Projects

Anchorage, AK
(907) 269-4957

Tuscaloosa, AL
(205) 348-3033

Little Rock, AR
(501) 682-4522

Phoenix, AZ
(602) 542-1695

Sacramento, CA
(916) 263-2856

Fort Collins, CO
(970) 491-6151

Wethersfield, CT
(860) 566-4550

Washington, DC
(202) 541-3727

Wilmington, DE
(302) 761-8219

Tampa, FL
(813) 974-9962

Atlanta, GA
(404) 894-2643

Tiyam, GU
9-1-(671) 475-1101

Honolulu, HI
(808) 586-9100

Des Moines, IA
(515) 281-7629

Boise, ID
(208) 426-3283

Chicago, IL
(312) 814-2337

Indianapolis, IN
(317) 232-2688

Topeka, KS
(785) 296-2251

Frankfort, KY
(502) 564-6895

Baton Rouge, LA
(225) 342-9601

West Newton, MA
(617) 727-3982

Laurel, MD
(410) 880-4970

Augusta, ME
(207) 624-6400

Lansing, MI
(517) 322-1809

Saint Paul, MN
(651) 284-5060

Jefferson City, MO
(573) 751-3403

Pearl, MS
(601) 939-2047

Helena, MT
(406) 444-6418

Raleigh, NC
(919) 807-2905

Bismarck, ND
(701) 328-5188

Lincoln, NE
(402) 471-4717

Concord, NH
(603) 271-2024

Trenton, NJ
(609) 292-3923

Santa Fe, NM
(505) 827-4230

Henderson, NV
(702) 486-9140

Albany, NY
(518) 457-2238

Columbus, OH
(614) 644-2631

Oklahoma City, OK
(405) 528-1500

Salem, OR
(503) 378-3272

Indiana, PA
(724) 357-2396

Hato Rey, PR
(787) 754-2171

Providence, RI
(401) 222-2438

Columbia, SC
(803) 734-9614

Brookings, SD
(605) 688-4101

Nashville, TN
(615) 741-7036

Austin, TX
(512) 804-4640

Salt Lake City, UT
(801) 530-6901

Richmond, VA
(804) 786-6359

Christiansted St. Croix, VI
(809) 772-1315

Montpelier, VT
(802) 828-2765

Olympia, WA
(360) 902-5638

Madison, WI
(608) 266-9383

Waukesha, WI
(262) 523-3044

Charleston, WV
(304) 558-7890

Cheyenne, WY
(307) 777-7786

Lead in Construction

Lead in Construction

U.S. Department of Labor

Occupational Safety and Health Administration

OSHA 3142-09R

2003

This informational book provides a general overview of a particular topic related to OSHA standards. It does not alter or determine compliance responsibilities in OSHA standards or the *Occupational Safety and Health Act of 1970*. Because interpretations and enforcement policy may change over time, you should consult current OSHA administrative interpretations and decisions by the Occupational Safety and Health Review Commission and the Courts for additional guidance on OSHA compliance requirements.

This information is available to sensory impaired individuals upon request. Voice phone: (202) 693-1999; teletypewriter (TTY) number: (877) 889-5627.

Contents - Lead in Construction

Health Hazards of Lead Exposure

Pure lead (Pb) is a heavy metal at room temperature and pressure. A basic chemical element, it can combine with various other substances to form numerous lead compounds.

Lead has been poisoning workers for thousands of years. Lead can damage the central nervous system, cardiovascular system, reproductive system, hematological system, and kidneys. When absorbed into the body in high enough doses, lead can be toxic.

In addition, workers' lead exposure can harm their children's development.

Short-term (acute) overexposure — as short as days — can cause acute encephalopathy, a condition affecting the brain that develops quickly into seizures, coma, and death from cardiorespiratory arrest. Short-term occupational exposures of this type are highly unusual but not impossible.

Extended, long-term (chronic) overexposure can result in severe damage to the central nervous system, particularly the brain. It can also damage the blood-forming, urinary, and reproductive systems. There is no sharp dividing line between rapidly developing acute effects of lead and chronic effects that take longer to develop.

SYMPTOMS OF CHRONIC OVEREXPOSURE

Some of the common symptoms include:

- Loss of appetite;
- Constipation;
- Nausea;
- Excessive tiredness;
- Headache;
- Fine tremors;
- Colic with severe abdominal pain;
- Metallic taste in the mouth;
- Weakness;
- Nervous irritability;
- Hyperactivity;

- Muscle and joint pain or soreness;
- Anxiety;
- Pallor;
- Insomnia;
- Numbness; and
- Dizziness.

REPRODUCTIVE RISKS

Lead is toxic to both male and female reproductive systems. Lead can alter the structure of sperm cells and there is evidence of miscarriage and stillbirth in women exposed to lead or whose partners have been exposed. Children born to parents who were exposed to excess lead levels are more likely to have birth defects, mental retardation, or behavioral disorders or to die during the first year of childhood.

Workers who desire medical advice about reproductive issues related to lead should contact qualified medical personnel to arrange for a job evaluation and medical followup — particularly if they are pregnant or actively seeking to have a child. Employers whose employees may be exposed to lead and who have been contacted by employees with concerns about reproductive issues must make medical examinations and consultations available.

CHELATING AGENTS

Under certain limited circumstances, a physician may prescribe special drugs called chelating agents to reduce the amount of lead absorbed in body tissues. Using chelation as a preventive measure — that is, to lower blood level but continue to expose a worker — is prohibited and therapeutic or diagnostic chelations of lead that are required must be done under the supervision of a licensed physician in a clinical setting, with thorough and appropriate medical monitoring. The employee must be notified in writing before treatment of potential consequences and allowed to obtain a second opinion.

Worker Exposure

Lead is most commonly absorbed into the body by inhalation. When workers breathe in lead as a dust, fume, or mist, their lungs and upper respiratory tract absorb it into the body. They can also absorb lead through the digestive system if it enters the mouth and is ingested.

A significant portion of the lead inhaled or ingested gets into the bloodstream. Once in the bloodstream, lead circulates through the body and is stored in various organs and body tissues. Some of this lead is filtered out of the body quickly and excreted, but some remains in the blood and tissues. As exposure continues, the amount stored will increase if the body absorbs more lead than it excretes. The lead stored in the tissue can slowly cause irreversible damage, first to individual cells, then to organs and whole body systems.

Construction Workers and Lead Exposure

HOW LEAD IS USED

In construction, lead is used frequently for roofs, cornices, tank linings, and electrical conduits. In plumbing, soft solder, used chiefly for soldering tinplate and copper pipe joints, is an alloy of lead and tin. Soft solder has been banned for many uses in the United States. In addition, the Consumer Product Safety Commission bans the use of lead-based paint in residences. Because lead-based paint inhibits the rusting and corrosion of iron and steel, however, lead continues to be used on bridges, railways, ships, lighthouses, and other steel structures, although substitute coatings are available.

Construction projects vary in their scope and potential for exposing workers to lead and other hazards. Projects such as removing paint from a few interior residential doors may involve limited exposure. Others projects, however, may involve removing or stripping substantial quantities of lead-based paints on large bridges and other structures.

MOST VULNERABLE WORKERS

Workers potentially at risk for lead exposure include those involved in iron work; demolition work; painting; lead-based paint abatement; plumbing; heating and air conditioning maintenance and repair; electrical work; and carpentry, renovation, and remodeling work. Plumbers, welders, and painters are among those workers most exposed to lead. Significant lead exposures also can arise from removing paint from surfaces previously coated with lead-based paint such as bridges, residences being renovated, and structures being demolished or salvaged. With the increase in highway work, bridge repair, residential lead abatement, and residential remodeling, the potential for exposure to lead-based paint has become more common.

Workers at the highest risk of lead exposure are those involved in:

- Abrasive blasting and
- Welding, cutting, and burning on steel structures.

Other operations with the potential to expose workers to lead include:

- Lead burning;
- Using lead-containing mortar;
- Power tool cleaning without dust collection systems;
- Rivet busting;
- Cleanup activities where dry expendable abrasives are used;
- Movement and removal of abrasive blasting enclosures;
- Manual dry scraping and sanding;
- Manual demolition of structures;
- Heat-gun applications;
- Power tool cleaning with dust collection systems; and
- Spray painting with lead-based paint.

OSHA's Lead Standard

OSHA's Lead Standard for the Construction Industry, Title 29 Code of Federal Regulations 1926.62, covers lead in a variety of forms, including metallic lead, all inorganic lead compounds, and organic lead soaps.

EXPOSURE LIMITS

The standard establishes maximum limits of exposure to lead for all workers covered, including a permissible exposure limit (PEL) and action level (AL).

The PEL sets the maximum worker exposure to lead: 50 micrograms of lead per cubic meter of air (50µg/m3) averaged over an eight-hour period. If employees are exposed to lead for more than eight hours in a workday, their allowable exposure as a TWA for that day must be reduced according to this formula:

Employee exposure (in µg/m3) = 400 divided by the hours worked in the day.

The AL, regardless of respirator use, is an airborne concentration of 30μg/m3, averaged over an eight-hour period. The AL is the level at which an employer must begin specific compliance activities outlined in the standard.

APPLICABILITY TO CONSTRUCTION

OSHA's lead in construction standard applies to all construction work where an employee may be exposed to lead. All work related to construction, alteration, or repair, including painting and decorating, is included. Under this standard, construction includes, but is not limited to:

- Demolition or salvage of structures where lead or materials containing lead are present;
- Removal or encapsulation of materials containing lead;
- New construction, alteration, repair, or renovation of structures, substrates, or portions or materials containing lead;
- Installation of products containing lead;
- Lead contamination from emergency cleanup;
- Transportation, disposal, storage, or containment of lead or materials containing lead where construction activities are performed; and
- Maintenance operations associated with these construction activities.

Employer Responsibilities

WORKER PROTECTIONS

Employers of construction workers are responsible for developing and implementing a worker protection program. At a minimum, the employer's worker protection program for employees exposed to lead above the PEL should include:

- Hazard determination, including exposure assessment;
- Medical surveillance and provisions for medical removal;
- Job-specific compliance programs;
- Engineering and work practice controls;
- Respiratory protection;
- Protective clothing and equipment;

- Housekeeping;
- Hygiene facilities and practices;
- Signs;
- Employee information and training; and
- Recordkeeping.

Because lead is a cumulative and persistent toxic substance and health effects may result from exposure over prolonged periods, employers must use these precautions where feasible to minimize employee exposure to lead. The employer should, as needed, consult a qualified safety and health professional to develop and implement an effective, site-specific worker protection program. These professionals may work independently or may be associated with an insurance carrier, trade organization, or onsite consultation program.

ELEMENTS OF A COMPLIANCE PROGRAM

For each job where employee exposure exceeds the PEL, the employer must establish and implement a written compliance program to reduce employee exposure to the PEL or below. The compliance program must provide for frequent and regular inspections of job sites, materials, and equipment by a competent person. Written programs, which must be reviewed and updated at least every six months, must include:

- A description of each activity in which lead is emitted (such as equipment used, material involved, controls in place, crew size, employee job responsibilities, operating procedures, and maintenance practices);
- The means to be used to achieve compliance and engineering plans and studies used to determine the engineering controls selected where they are required;
- Information on the technology considered to meet the PEL;
- Air monitoring data that document the source of lead emissions;
- A detailed schedule for implementing the program, including copies of documentation (such as purchase orders for equipment, construction contracts);
- A work practice program;
- An administrative control schedule, if applicable; and
- Arrangements made among contractors on multi-contractor sites to inform employees of potential lead exposure.

Hazard Assessment

An employer is required to conduct an initial employee exposure assessment of whether employees are exposed to lead at or above the AL based on:

- Any information, observation, or calculation that indicates employee exposure to lead;
- Any previous measurements of airborne lead; and
- Any employee complaints of symptoms attributable to lead exposure.

Objective data and historical measurements of lead may be used to satisfy the standard's initial monitoring requirements.

INITIAL EMPLOYEE EXPOSURE ASSESSMENT

Initial monitoring may be limited to a representative sample of those employees exposed to the greatest concentrations of airborne lead. Representative exposure sampling is permitted when there are a number of employees performing the same job, with lead exposure of similar duration and level, under essentially the same conditions. For employees engaged in similar work, the standard requires that the members of the group reasonably expected to have the highest exposure levels be monitored. This result is then attributed to the other employees of the group.

The employer must establish and maintain an accurate record documenting the nature and relevancy of previous exposure data. Instead of performing initial monitoring, the employer may in some cases rely on objective data that demonstrate that a particular lead-containing material or product cannot result in employee exposure at or above the action level when it is processed, used, or handled.

BIOLOGICAL MONITORING TESTS

Analysis of blood lead samples must be conducted by an OSHA-approved lab and be accurate (to a confidence level of 95 percent) within plus or minus 15 percent, or 6 μg/dl, whichever is greater. If an employee's airborne lead level is at or above the AL for more than 30 days in any consecutive 12 months, the employer must make biological monitoring available on the following schedule:

- At least every two months for the first six months and every six months thereafter for employees exposed at or above the action level for more than 30 days annually;

- At least every two months for employees whose last blood sampling and analysis indicated a blood lead level at or above 40 μg/dl; and
- At least monthly while an employee is removed from exposure due an elevated blood lead level.

PENDING EMPLOYEE EXPOSURE ASSESSMENT

Until the employer performs an exposure assessment and documents that employees are not exposed above the PEL, OSHA requires some degree of interim protection for employees. This means providing respiratory protection, protective work clothing and equipment, hygiene facilities, biological monitoring, and training—as specified by the standards—for certain tasks prone to produce high exposure. These include:

- Manual demolition of structures such as dry wall, manual scraping, manual sanding, and use of a heat gun where lead-containing coatings or paints are present;
- Power tool cleaning with or without local exhaust ventilation;
- Spray painting with lead-containing paint;
- Lead burning;
- Use of lead-containing mortar;
- Abrasive blasting, rivet busting, welding, cutting, or torch-burning on any structure where lead-containing coatings or paint are present;
- Abrasive blasting enclosure movement and removal;
- Cleanup of activities where dry expendable abrasives are used; and
- Any other task the employer believes may cause exposures in excess of the PEL.

TEST RESULTS SHOWING NO OVEREXPOSURES

If the initial assessment indicates that no employee is exposed above the AL, the employer may discontinue monitoring. Further exposure testing is not required unless there is a change in processes or controls that may result in additional employees being exposed to lead at or above the AL, or may result in employees already exposed at or above the AL being exposed above the PEL. The employer must keep a written record of the determination, including the date, location within the work site, and the name and social security number of each monitored employee.

EMPLOYEE NOTIFICATION OF MONITORING RESULTS

The employer must notify each employee in writing of employee exposure assessment results within five working days of receiving them. Whenever the results indicate that the representative employee exposure, without the use of respirators, is above the PEL, the employer must include a written notice stating that the employee's exposure exceeded the PEL and describing corrective action taken or to be taken to reduce exposure to or below the PEL.

Medical Surveillance

When an employee's airborne exposure is at or above the AL for more than 30 days in any consecutive 12 months, an immediate medical consultation is required when the employee notifies the employer that he or she:

- Has developed signs or symptoms commonly associated with lead-related disease;
- Has demonstrated difficulty in breathing during respirator use or a fit test;
- Desires medical advice concerning the effects of past or current lead exposure on the employee's ability to have a healthy child; and
- Is under medical removal and has a medically appropriate need.

MEDICAL EXAMS

The best indicator of personal lead exposure is through a blood test to indicate elevated blood lead levels. A medical exam must also include:

- Detailed work and medical histories, with particular attention to past lead exposure (occupational and nonoccupational), personal habits (smoking and hygiene), and past gastrointestinal, hematologic, renal, cardiovascular, reproductive, and neurological problems;
- A thorough physical exam, with particular attention to gums, teeth, hematologic, gastrointestinal, renal, cardiovascular, and neurological systems; evaluation of lung function if respirators are used;
- A blood pressure measurement;
- A blood sample and analysis to determine blood lead level;
- Hemoglobin and hematocrit determinations, red cell indices, and an exam of peripheral smear morphology; and

- Zinc protopor-phyrin; blood urea nitrogen; and serum creatinine;
- A routine urinalysis with microscopic exam; and
- Any lab or other test the examining physician deems necessary.

INFORMATION FOR THE EXAMINING PHYSICIAN

The employer must provide all examining physicians with a copy of the lead in construction standard, including all appendices, a description of the affected employees duties as they relate to the employee's exposure, the employees lead exposure level or anticipated exposure level, a description of personal protective equipment used or to be used, prior blood lead determinations, and all prior written medical opinions for the employee.

WHEN MONITORING SHOWS NO EMPLOYEE EXPOSURES ABOVE THE AL

Employers must make available, at no cost to the employee, initial medical surveillance for employees exposed to lead on the job at or above the action level on any one day per year. This initial medical surveillance consists of biological monitoring in the form of blood sampling and analysis for lead and zinc protoporyrin (ZPP) levels. In addition, a medical surveillance program with biological monitoring must be made available to any employee exposed at or above the action level for more than 30 days in any consecutive 12 months.

AFTER THE MEDICAL EXAMINATION

Employers must obtain and provide the employee a copy of a written opinion from each examining or consulting physician that contains only information related to occupational exposure to lead and must include:

- Whether the employee has any detected medical condition that would increase the health risk from lead exposure;
- Any special protective measures or limitations on the worker's exposure to lead;
- Any limitation on respirator use; and
- Results of the blood lead determinations. In addition, the written statement may include a statement that the physician has informed the employee of the results of the consultation or medical examination and any medical condition that may require further examination or treatment.

The employer must instruct the physician that findings, including lab results or diagnoses unrelated to the worker's lead exposure, must not be revealed to the employer or included in the written opinion to the employer. The employer must also instruct the physician to advise employees of any medical condition, occupational or non-occupational, that necessitates further evaluation or treatment. In addition, some states also require laboratories and health care providers to report cases of elevated blood lead concentrations to their state health departments.

Medical Removal Provisions

Temporary medical removal can result from an elevated blood level or a written medical opinion. More specifically, the employer is required to remove from work an employee with a lead exposure at or above the AL each time periodic and follow-up (within two weeks of the periodic test) blood sampling tests indicate that the employee's blood level is at or above 50 µg /dl. The employer also must remove from work an employee with lead exposure at or above the AL each time a final medical determination indicates that the employee needs reduced lead exposure for medical reasons. If the physician who is implementing the employer's medical program makes a final written opinion recommending the employee's removal or other special protective measures, the employer must implement the physician's recommendation.

For an employee removed from exposure to lead at or above the AL due to a blood lead level at or above 50 µg/dl, the employer may return that employee to former job status when two consecutive blood sampling tests indicate that the employee's blood lead level is below 40 µg /dl. For an employee removed from exposure to lead due to a final medical determination, the employee must be returned when a subsequent final medical determination results in a medical finding, determination, or opinion that the employee no longer has a detected medical condition that places the employee at increased risk of lead exposure.

The employer must remove any limitations placed on employees or end any special protective measures when a subsequent final medical determination indicates they are no longer necessary. If the former position no longer exists, the employee is returned consistent with whatever job assignment discretion the employer would have had if no removal occurred.

WORKER PROTECTIONS AND BENEFITS

The employer must provide up to 18 months of medical removal protection (MRP) benefits each time an employee is removed from lead exposure or medically limited. As long as the position/job exists, the employer must maintain the earnings, seniority, and other employment rights and benefits as though the employee had not been removed from the job or otherwise medically limited. The employer may condition medical removal protection benefits on the employees participation in followup medical surveillance.

If a removed employee files a workers compensation claim or other compensation for lost wages due to a lead-related disability, the employer must continue medical removal protection benefits until the claim is resolved. However, the employers MRP benefits obligation will be reduced by the amount that the employee receives from these sources. Also, the employer's MRP benefits obligation will be reduced by any income the employee receives from employment with another employer made possible by virtue of the employee's removal.

RECORDS REQUIREMENTS INVOLVING MEDICAL REMOVAL

In the case of medical removal, the employer's records must include:

- The worker's name and social security number,
- The date of each occasion that the worker was removed from current exposure to lead,
- The date when the worker was returned to the former job status,
- A brief explanation of how each removal was or is being accomplished, and
- A statement indicating whether the reason for the removal was an elevated blood lead level.

Recordkeeping

EMPLOYER REQUIREMENTS

The employer must maintain any employee exposure and medical records to document ongoing employee exposure, medical monitoring, and medical removal of workers. This data provides a baseline to evaluate the employee's health properly. Employees or former employees, their designated representatives, and

OSHA must have access to exposure and medical records in accordance with 29 CFR 1910.1020. Rules of agency practice and procedure governing OSHA access to employee medical records are found in 29 CFR 1913.10.

EXPOSURE ASSESSMENT RECORDS

The employer must establish and maintain an accurate record of all monitoring and other data used to conduct employee exposure assessments as required by this standard and in accordance with 29 CFR 1910.1020. The exposure assessment records must include:

- The dates, number, duration, location, and results of each sample taken, including a description of the sampling procedure used to determine representative employee exposure;
- A description of the sampling and analytical methods used and evidence of their accuracy;
- The type of respiratory protection worn, if any;
- The name, social security number, and job classification of the monitored employee and all others whose exposure the mea-surement represents; and
- Environmental variables that could affect the measurement of employee exposure.

MEDICAL SURVEILLANCE RECORDS

The employer must maintain an accurate record for each employee subject to medical surveillance, including:

- The name, social security number, and description of the employees duties;
- A copy of the physicians written opinions;
- The results of any airborne exposure monitoring done for the employee and provided to the physician; and
- Any employee medical complaints related to lead exposure.

In addition, the employer must keep or ensure that the examining physician keeps the following medical records:

- A copy of the medical examination results including medical and work history;

- A description of the laboratory procedures and a copy of any guidelines used to interpret the test results; and
- A copy of the results of biological monitoring.

The employer or physician or both must maintain medical records in accordance with 29 CFR 1910.1020.

DOCUMENTS FOR EMPLOYEES SUBJECT TO MEDICAL REMOVAL

The employer must maintain — for at least the duration of employment — an accurate record for each employee subject to medical removal, including:

- The name and social security number of the employee;
- The date on each occasion that the employee was removed from current exposure to lead and the corresponding date which the employee was returned to former job status;
- A brief explanation of how each removal was or is being accomplished; and
- A statement about each removal indicating whether the reason for removal was an elevated blood level.

EMPLOYER REQUIREMENTS RELATED TO OBJECTIVE DATA

The employer must establish and maintain an accurate record documenting the nature and relevancy of objective data relied on to assess initial employee exposure in lieu of exposure monitoring. The employer must maintain the record of objective data relied on for at least 30 years.

DOCUMENTS FOR OSHA AND NIOSH REVIEW

The employer must make all records— including exposure monitoring, objective data, medical removal, and medical records—available upon request to affected employees, former employees, and their designated representatives and to the OSHA Assistant Secretary and the Director of the National Institute for Occupational Safety and Health (NIOSH) for examination and copying in accordance with 29 CFR 1910.1020.

WHEN CLOSING A BUSINESS

When an employer ceases to do business, the successor employer must receive and retain all required records. If no successor is available, these records must be sent to the Director of NIOSH.

Exposure Reduction and Employee Protection

The most effective way to protect workers is to minimize their exposure through engineering controls, good work practices and training, and use of personal protective clothing and equipment, including respirators, where required. The employer needs to designate a competent person capable of identifying existing and predictable lead hazards and who is authorized to take prompt corrective measures to eliminate such problems. The employer should, as needed, consult a qualified safety and health professional to develop and implement an effective worker protection program. These professionals may work independently or may be associated with an insurance carrier, trade organization, or onsite consultation program.

Engineering Controls

Engineering measures include local and general exhaust ventilation, process and equipment modification, material substitution, component replacement, and isolation or automation. Examples of recommended engineering controls that can help reduce worker exposure to lead are described as follows.

EXHAUST VENTILATION

Equip power tools used to remove lead-based paint with dust collection shrouds or other attachments so that paint is exhausted through a high-efficiency particulate air (HEPA) vacuum system. For operations such as welding, cutting/burning, or heating, use local exhaust ventilation. Use HEPA vacuums during cleanup operations.

For abrasive blasting operations, build a containment structure that is designed to optimize the flow of clean ventilation air past the workers' breathing zones. This will help reduce the exposure to airborne lead and increase visibility. Maintain the affected area under negative pressure to reduce the chances that lead dust will contaminate areas outside the enclosure. Equip the containment structure with an adequately sized dust collector to control emissions of particulate matter into the environment.

ENCLOSURE OR ENCAPSULATION

One way to reduce the lead inhalation or ingestion hazard posed by lead-based paint is to encapsulate it with a material that bonds to the surface, such as acrylic or epoxy coating or flexible wall coverings. Another option is to enclose it using systems such as gypsum wallboard, plywood paneling, and aluminum, vinyl, or wood exterior siding. Floors coated with lead-based paint can be covered using vinyl tile or linoleum.

The building owner or other responsible person should oversee the custodial and maintenance staffs and contractors during all activities involving enclosed or encapsulated lead-based paint. This will minimize the potential for an inadvertent lead release during maintenance, renovation, or demolition.

SUBSTITUTION

Choose materials and chemicals that do not contain lead for construction projects. Among the options are:

- Use zinc-containing primers covered by an epoxy intermediate coat and polyurethane topcoat instead of lead-containing coatings.
- Substitute mobile hydraulic shears for torch cutting under certain circumstances.
- Consider surface preparation equipment such as needle guns with multiple reciprocating needles completely enclosed within an adjustable shroud, instead of abrasive blasting under certain conditions. The shroud captures dust and debris at the cutting edge and can be equipped with a HEPA vacuum filtration with a self-drumming feature. One such commercial unit can remove lead-based paint from flat steel and concrete surfaces, outside edges, inside corners, and pipes.
- Choose chemical strippers in lieu of hand scraping with a heat gun for work on building exteriors, surfaces involving carvings or molding, or intricate iron work. Chemical removal generates less airborne lead dust. (Be aware, however, that these strippers themselves can be hazardous and that the employer must review the material safety data sheets (MSDSs) for these stripping agents to obtain information on their hazards.)

COMPONENT REPLACEMENT

Replace lead-based painted building components such as windows, doors, and trim with new components free of lead-containing paint. Another option is to remove the paint offsite and then repaint the components with zinc-based paint before replacing them.

PROCESS OR EQUIPMENT MODIFICATION

When applying lead paints or other lead-containing coatings, use a brush or roller rather than a sprayer. This application method introduces little or no paint mist into the air to present a lead inhalation hazard. (Note that there is a ban on the use of lead-based paint in residential housing.)

Use non-silica-containing abrasives such as steel or iron shot/grit sand instead of sand in abrasive blasting operations when practical. The free silica portion of the dust presents a respiratory health hazard.

When appropriate for the conditions, choose blasting techniques that are less dusty than open-air abrasive blasting. These include hydro- or wet-blasting using high-pressure water with or without an abrasive or surrounding the blast nozzle with a ring of water, and vacuum blasting where a vacuum hood for material removal is positioned around the exterior of the blasting nozzle.

When using a heat gun to remove lead-based paints in residential housing units, be sure it is of the flameless electrical softener type. Heat guns should have electronically controlled temperature settings to allow usage below 700 degrees F. Equip heat guns with various nozzles to cover all common applications and to limit the size of the heated work area.

When using abrasive blasting with a vacuum hood on exterior building surfaces, ensure that the configuration of the heads on the blasting nozzle match the configuration of the substrate so that the vacuum is effective in containing debris.

Ensure that HEPA vacuum cleaners have the appropriate attachments for use on unusual surfaces. Proper use of brushes of various sizes, crevice and angular tools, when needed, will enhance the quality of the HEPA-vacuuming process and help reduce the amount of lead dust released into the air.

ISOLATION

Although it is not feasible to enclose and ventilate some abrasive blasting operations completely, it is possible to isolate many operations to help reduce the potential for lead exposure. Isolation consists of keeping employees not involved in the blasting operations as far away from the work area as possible, reducing the risk of exposure.

Housekeeping and Personal Hygiene

Lead is a cumulative and persistent toxic substance that poses a serious health risk. A rigorous housekeeping program and the observance of basic personal hygiene practices will minimize employee exposure to lead. In addition, these two elements of the worker protection program help prevent workers from taking lead-contaminated dust out of the worksite and into their homes where it can extend the workers' exposures and potentially affect their families' health.

HOUSEKEEPING PRACTICES

An effective housekeeping program involves a regular schedule to remove accumulations of lead dust and lead-containing debris. The schedule should be adapted to exposure conditions at a particular worksite. OSHA's Lead Standard for Construction requires employers to maintain all surfaces as free of lead contamination as practicable. Vacuuming lead dust with HEPA-filtered equipment or wetting the dust with water before sweeping are effective control measures. Compressed air may not be used to remove lead from contaminated surfaces unless a ventilation system is in place to capture the dust generated by the compressed air.

In addition, put all lead-containing debris and contaminated items accumulated for disposal into sealed, impermeable bags or other closed impermeable containers. Label bags and containers as lead-containing waste. These measures provide additional help in controlling exposure.

PERSONAL HYGIENE PRACTICES

Emphasize workers' personal hygiene such as washing their hands and face after work and before eating to minimize their exposure to lead. Provide and ensure that workers use washing facilities. Provide clean change areas and readily accessible eating areas. If possible, provide a parking area where cars will not be contaminated with lead. These measures:

- Reduce workers' exposure to lead and the likelihood that they will ingest lead,
- Ensure that the exposure does not extend beyond the worksite,
- Reduce the movement of lead from the worksite, and
- Provide added protection to employees and their families.

CHANGE AREAS

The employer must provide a clean change area for employees whose airborne exposure to lead is above the PEL. The area must be equipped with storage facilities for street clothes and a separate area with facilities for the removal and storage of lead-contaminated protective work clothing and equipment. This separation prevents cross contamination of the employee's street and work clothing.

Employees must use a clean change area for taking off street clothes, suiting up in clean protective work clothing, donning respirators before beginning work, and dressing in street clothes after work. No lead-contaminated items should enter this area.

Work clothing must not be worn away from the jobsite. Under no circumstances should lead-contaminated work clothes be laundered at home or taken from the worksite, except to be laundered professionally or for disposal following applicable federal, state, and local regulations.

SHOWERS AND WASHING FACILITIES

When feasible, showers must be provided for use by employees whose airborne exposure to lead is above the permissible exposure limit so they can shower before leaving the worksite. Where showers are provided, employees must change out of their work clothes and shower before changing into their street clothes and leaving the worksite. If employees do not change into clean clothing before leaving the worksite, they may contaminate their homes and automobiles with lead dust, extending their exposure and exposing other members of their household to lead.

In addition, employers must provide adequate washing facilities for their workers. These facilities must be close to the worksite and furnished with water, soap, and clean towels so employees can remove lead contamination from their skin.

Contaminated water from washing facilities and showers must be disposed of in accordance with applicable local, state, or federal regulations.

PERSONAL PRACTICES

The employer must ensure that employees do not enter lunchroom facilities or eating areas with protective work clothing or equipment unless surface lead dust has been removed. HEPA vacuuming and use of a downdraft booth are examples of cleaning methods that limit the dispersion of lead dust from contaminated work clothing.

In all areas where employees are exposed to lead above the PEL, employees must observe the prohibition on the presence and consumption or use of food, beverages, tobacco products, and cosmetics. Employees whose airborne exposure to lead is above the PEL must wash their hands and face before eating, drinking, smoking, or applying cosmetics.

END-OF-DAY PROCEDURES

Employers must ensure that workers who are exposed to lead above the permissible exposure limit follow these procedures at the end of their workday:

- Place contaminated clothes, including work shoes and personal protective equipment to be cleaned, laundered, or disposed of, in a properly labeled closed container.
- Take a shower and wash their hair. Where showers are not provided, employees must wash their hands and face at the end of the workshift.
- Change into street clothes in clean change areas.

Protective Clothing and Equipment

EMPLOYER REQUIREMENTS

Employers must provide workers who are exposed to lead above the PEL or for whom the possibility of skin or eye irritation exists with clean, dry protective work clothing and equipment that are appropriate for the hazard. Employers must provide these items at no cost to employees. Appropriate protective work clothing and equipment used on construction sites includes:

- Coveralls or other full-body work clothing;
- Gloves, hats, and shoes or disposable shoe coverlets;
- Vented goggles or face shields with protective spectacles or goggles;
- Welding or abrasive blasting helmets; and
- Respirators.

Clean work clothing must be issued daily for employees whose exposure levels to lead are above 200 μg/m3, weekly if exposures are above the PEL but at or below 200 μg/m3 or where the possibility of skin or eye irritation exists.

HANDLING CONTAMINATED PROTECTIVE CLOTHING

Workers must not be allowed to leave the worksite wearing lead-contaminated protective clothing or equipment. This is an essential step in reducing the movement of lead contamination from the workplace into the worker's home and provides added protection for employees and their families.

Disposable coveralls and separate shoe covers may be used, if appropriate, to avoid the need for laundering. Workers must remove protective clothing in change rooms provided for that purpose.

Employers must ensure that employees leave the respirator use area to wash their faces and respirator facepieces as necessary. In addition, employers may require their employees to use HEPA vacuuming, damp wiping, or another suitable cleaning method before removing a respirator to clear loose particle contamination on the respirator and at the face-mask seal.

Place contaminated clothing that is to be cleaned, laundered, or disposed of by the employer in closed containers. Label containers with the warning: "Caution: Clothing contaminated with lead. Do not remove dust by blowing or shaking. Dispose of lead-contaminated wash water in accordance with applicable local, state, or federal regulations."

Workers responsible for handling contaminated clothing, including those in laundry services or subcontractors, must be informed in writing of the potential health hazard of lead exposure. At no time shall lead be removed from protective clothing or equipment by brushing, shaking, or blowing. These actions disperse the lead into the work area.

PREVENTING HEAT STRESS

Workers wearing protective clothing, particularly in hot environments or within containment structures, can face a risk from heat stress if proper control measures are not used.

Heat stress is caused by several interacting factors, including environmental conditions, type of protective clothing worn, the work activity required and anticipated work rate, and individual employee characteristics such as age, weight, and fitness level. When heat stress is a concern, the employer should choose lighter, less insulating protective clothing over heavier clothing, as long as it provides adequate protection. Other measures the employer can take include: discussing the possibility of heat stress and its signs and symptoms with all workers; using appropriate work/rest regimens; and providing heat stress monitoring that includes measuring employees' heart rates, body temperatures, and weight loss. Employers must provide a source of water or electrolyte drink in a non-contaminated eating and drinking area close to the work area so workers can drink often throughout the day. Workers must wash their hands and face before drinking any fluid if their airborne exposure is above the PEL.

Respiratory Protection

Although engineering and work practice controls are the primary means of protecting workers from exposure to lead, source control at construction sites sometimes is insufficient to control exposure. In these cases, airborne lead concentrations may be high or may vary widely. Respirators often must be used to supplement engineering controls and work practices to reduce worker lead exposures below the PEL. When respirators are required, employers must provide them at no cost to workers.

The standard requires that respirators be used during periods when an employee's exposure to lead exceeds the PEL, including

- Periods necessary to install or implement engineering or work practice controls, and
- Work operations for which engineering and work practice controls are insufficient to reduce employee exposures to or below the PEL.

Respirators also must be provided upon employee request. A requested respirator is included as a requirement to provide increased protection for those employees who wish to reduce their lead burden below what is required by the standard, particularly if they intend to have children in the near future. In addition, respirators must be used when performing previously indicated high exposure or "trigger" tasks, before completion of the initial assessment.

PROVIDING ADEQUATE RESPIRATORY PROTECTION

Before any employee first starts wearing a respirator in the work environment, the employer must perform a fit test. For all employees wearing negative or positive pressure tight-fitting facepiece respirators, the employer must perform either qualitative or quantitative fit tests using an OSHA-accepted fit testing protocol. In addition, employees must be fit tested whenever a different respirator facepiece is used, and at least annually thereafter.

Where daily airborne exposure to lead exceeds 50 μg/m3, affected workers must don respirators before entering the work area and should not remove them until they leave the high-exposure area or have completed a decontamination procedure. Employers must assure that the respirator issued to the employee is selected and fitted properly to ensure minimum leakage through the facepiece-to-face seal.

RESPIRATORY PROTECTION PROGRAMS

When respirators are required at a worksite, the employer must establish a respiratory protection program in accordance with the OSHA standard on respiratory protection, 29 CFR 1910.134. At a minimum, an acceptable respirator program for lead must include:

- Procedures for selecting respirators appropriate to the hazard;
- Fit testing procedures;
- Procedures for proper use of respirators in routine and reasonably foreseeable emergency situations, including cartridge change schedules;
- Procedures and schedules for cleaning, disinfecting, storing, inspecting, repairing, discarding, and otherwise maintaining respirators;
- Training of employees in the respiratory hazard to which they are potentially exposed during routine and emergency situations;
- Training of employees in the proper use of respirators, including putting on and removing them, any limitations of their use, and their maintenance;
- Procedures for regularly evaluating the effectiveness of the program;

- Procedures to ensure air quality when supplied air is used;
- A written program and designation of a program administrator; and
- Recordkeeping procedures.

In addition, the construction industry lead standard stipulates medical evaluations of employees required to use respirators. If an employee has difficulty in breathing during a fit test or while using a respirator, the employer must make a medical examination available to that employee to determine whether he or she can wear a respirator safely.

SELECTING A RESPIRATOR

The employer must select the appropriate respirator from Table 1 of the lead standard, 29 CFR 1926.62(f)(3)(i). The employer must provide a powered air-purifying respirator when an employee chooses to use this respirator and it will provide the employee adequate protection. A NIOSH-certified respirator must be selected and used in compliance with the conditions of its certification. In addition, if exposure monitoring or experience indicates airborne exposures to contaminants other than lead such as silica, solvents, or polyurethane coatings, these exposures must be considered when selecting respiratory protection.

Select type CE respirators approved by NIOSH for abrasive blasting operations. Currently, there are two kinds of CE respirators with the following assigned protection factors (APFs): a continuous-flow respirator with a loose-fitting hood, APF 25; and a full facepiece supplied-air respirator operated in a positive-pressure mode, APF 2,000. (Note: OSHA recognizes Bullard Helmets, Models 77 and 88 (1995); Clemco Appollo, Models 20 and 60 (1997); and 3M Model 8100 (1998) as having APFs of 1,000.)

For any airline respirator, it is important to follow the manufacturer's instructions regarding air quality, air pressure, and inside diameter and length of hoses. Be aware that using longer hoses or smaller inside diameter hoses than the manufacturer specifies or hoses with bends or kinks may reduce or restrict the airflow to a respirator.

Employee Information and Training

The employer must inform employees about lead hazards according to the requirement of OSHAs Hazard Communication standard for the construction industry, 29 CFR 1926.59, including—but not limited to—the requirements for warning signs and labels, material safety data sheets (MSDSs), and employee information and training. (Refer to 29 CFR 1910.1200.)

PROGRAM REQUIREMENTS

Employers must institute an information and training program and ensure that all employees subject to exposure to lead or lead compounds at or above the action level on any day participate. Also covered under information and training are employees who may suffer skin or eye irritation from lead compounds. Initial training must be provided before the initial job assignment. Training must be repeated at least annually and, in brief summary, must include:

- The content of the OSHA lead standard and its appendices;
- The specific nature of operations that could lead to lead exposure above the action level;
- The purpose, proper selection, fit, use, and limitations of respirators;
- The purpose and a description of the medical surveillance program, and the medical removal protection program;
- Information concerning the adverse health effects associated with excessive lead exposure;
- The engineering and work practice controls associated with employees job assignments;
- The contents of any lead-related compliance plan in effect;
- Instructions to employees that chelating agents must not be used routinely to remove lead from their bodies and when necessary only under medical supervision and at the direction of a licensed physician; and
- The right to access records under "Access to Employee Exposure and Medical Records," 29 CFR 1910.1020.

All materials relating to the training program and a copy of the standard and its appendices must be made readily available to all affected employees.

WARNING SIGNS

Employers are required to post these warning signs in each work area where employee exposure to lead is above the PEL:

- WARNING

- LEAD WORK AREA
- POISON
- NO SMOKING OR EATING

All signs must be well lit and kept clean so that they are easily visible. Statements that contradict or detract from the signs meaning are prohibited. Signs required by other statutes, regulations, or ordinances, however, may be posted in addition to, or in combination with, this sign.

OSHA Assistance, Services, and Products

OSHA can provide extensive help through a variety of programs, including assistance about safety and health programs, state plans, workplace consultations, voluntary protection programs, strategic partnerships, alliances, and training and education. An overall commitment to workplace safety and health can add value to your business, to your workplace, and to your life.

How does safety and health management system assistance help employers and employees?

Working in a safe and healthful environment can stimulate innovation and creativity and result in increased performance and higher productivity. The key to a safe and healthful work environment is a comprehensive safety and health management system.

OSHA has electronic compliance assistance tools, or eTools, on its website that walks users through the steps required to develop a comprehensive safety and health program. The eTools are posted at www.osha.gov, and are based on guidelines that identify four general elements critical to a successful safety and health management system:

- Management leadership and employee involvement,
- Worksite analysis,
- Hazard prevention and control, and
- Safety and health training.

STATE PROGRAMS

The Occupational Safety and Health Act of 1970 (OSH Act) encourages states to develop and operate their own job safety and health plans. OSHA approves and monitors these plans and funds up to 50 percent of each program's operating costs. State plans must provide standards and enforcement programs, as well as voluntary compliance activities, that are at least as effective as federal OSHA's.

Currently, 26 states and territories have their own plans. Twenty-three cover both private and public (state and local government) employees and three states, Connecticut, New Jersey, and New York, cover only the public sector. For more information on state plans, see the list at the end of this publication, or visit OSHA's website at www.osha.gov.

CONSULTATION ASSISTANCE

Consultation assistance is available on request to employers who want help establishing and maintaining a safe and healthful workplace. Funded largely by OSHA, the service is provided at no cost to small employers and is delivered by state authorities through professional safety and health consultants.

SAFETY AND HEALTH ACHIEVEMENT RECOGNITION PROGRAM

Under the consultation program, certain exemplary employers may request participation in OSHAs Safety and Health Achievement Recognition Program (SHARP). Eligibility for participation includes, but is not limited to, receiving a full-service, comprehensive consultation visit, correcting all identified hazards, and developing an effective safety and health management system.

Employers accepted into SHARP may receive an exemption from programmed inspections (not complaint or accident investigation inspections) for 1 year initially, or 2 years upon renewal. For more information about consultation assistance, see the list of consultation projects at the end of this publication.

VOLUNTARY PROTECTION PROGRAMS

Voluntary Protection Programs (VPP) are designed to recognize outstanding achievements by companies that have developed and implemented effective safety and health management programs. There are three VPP programs: Star, Merit, and Demonstration. All are designed to

- Recognize who that have successfully developed and implemented effective and comprehensive safety and health management programs;

- Encourage these employers to continuously improve their safety and health management programs;
- Motivate other employers to achieve excellent safety and health results in the same outstanding way; and
- Establish a cooperative relationship between employers, employees, and OSHA.

VPP participation can bring many benefits to employers and employees, including fewer worker fatalities, injuries, and illnesses; lost-workday case rates generally 50 percent below industry averages; and lower workers compensation and other injury- and illness-related costs. In addition, many VPP sites report improved employee motivation to work safely, leading to a better quality of life at work; positive community recognition and interaction; further improvement and revitalization of already-good safety and health programs; and a positive relationship with OSHA.

After a site applies for the program, OSHA reviews an employers VPP application and conducts a VPP onsite evaluation to verify that the site's safety and health management programs are operating effectively. OSHA conducts onsite evaluations on a regular basis.

Sites participating in VPP are not scheduled for regular, programmed inspections. OSHA does, however, handle any employee complaints, serious accidents, or significant chemical releases that may occur at VPP sites according to routine enforcement procedures.

Additional information on VPP is available from OSHA regional offices listed at the end of this booklet. Also, see "Cooperative Programs" on OSHA's website.

COOPERATIVE PARTNERSHIPS

OSHA has learned firsthand that voluntary, cooperative partnerships with employers, employees, and unions can be a useful alternative to traditional enforcement and an effective way to reduce worker deaths, injuries, and illnesses. This is especially true when a partnership leads to the development and implementation of a comprehensive workplace safety and health management system.

ALLIANCE PROGRAM

Alliances enable organizations committed to workplace safety and health to collaborate with OSHA to prevent injuries and illnesses in the workplace. OSHA and its allies work together to reach out to, educate, and lead the nation's employers and their employees in improving and advancing workplace safety and health.

Alliances are open to all, including trade or professional organizations, businesses, labor organizations, educational institutions, and government agencies. In some cases, organizations may be building on existing relationships with OSHA through other cooperative programs.

There are few formal program requirements for alliances, which are less structured than other cooperative agreements, and the agreements do not include an enforcement component. However, OSHA and the participating organizations must define, implement, and meet a set of short- and long-term goals that fall into three categories: training and education; outreach and communication; and promotion of the national dialogue on workplace safety and health.

STRATEGIC PARTNERSHIP PROGRAM

OSHA Strategic Partnerships are agreements among labor, management, and government to improve workplace safety and health. These partnerships encourage, assist, and recognize the efforts of the partners to eliminate serious workplace hazards and achieve a high level of worker safety and health. Whereas OSHAs Consultation Program and VPP entail one-on-one relationships between OSHA and individual worksites, most strategic partnerships build cooperative relationships with groups of employers and employees.

For more information about this program, contact your nearest OSHA office or visit our website.

OCCUPATIONAL SAFETY AND HEALTH TRAINING

The OSHA Training Institute in Arlington Heights, Ill., provides basic and advanced training and education in safety and health for federal and state compliance officers, state consultants, other federal agency personnel, and private-sector employers, employees, and their representatives.

TRAINING GRANTS

OSHA awards grants to nonprofit organizations to provide safety and health training and education to employers and workers in the workplace. Grants often focus on high-risk activities or hazards or may help nonprofit organizations in training, education, and outreach.

OSHA expects each grantee to develop a program that addresses a safety and health topic named by OSHA, recruit workers and employers for the training, and conduct the training. Grantees are also expected to follow up with students to find out how they applied the training in their workplaces.

For more information contact OSHA Office of Training and Education, 2020 Arlington Heights Rd., Arlington Heights, IL 60005; or call (847) 297-4810.

OTHER ASSISTANCE MATERIALS

OSHA has a variety of materials and tools on its website at www.osha.gov. These include eTools such as Expert Advisors and Electronic Compliance Assistance Tools, information on specific health and safety topics, regulations, directives, publications, videos, and other information for employers and employees.

OSHA also has an extensive publications program. For a list of items, visit OSHA's website at www.osha.gov or contact the OSHA Publications Office, U.S. Department of Labor, 200 Constitution Avenue, NW, N-3101, Washington, DC 20210. Telephone (202) 6931888 or fax to (202) 693-2498.

In addition, OSHA's CD-ROM includes standards, interpretations, directives, and more. It is available for sale from the U.S. Government Printing Office. To order, write to the Superintendent of Documents, U.S. Government Printing Office, Washington, DC 20402, or phone (202) 512-1800.

IN CASE OF AN EMERGENCY OR TO FILE A COMPLAINT

To report an emergency, file a complaint, or seek OSHA advice, assistance, or products, call (800) 321-OSHA or contact your nearest OSHA regional office listed at the end of this publication. The teletypewriter (TTY) number is (877) 889-5627.

Employees can also file a complaint online and get more information on OSHA federal and state programs by visiting OSHA's website at www.osha.gov.

OSHA Regional Office Directory

Region I
(CT,* ME, MA, NH, RI, VT*)
JFK Federal Building, Room E340
Boston, MA 02203 (617) 565-9860

Region II
(NJ,* NY,* PR,* VI*)
201 Varick Street, Room 670
New York, NY 10014
(212) 337-2378

Region III
(DE, DC, MD,* PA,* VA,* WV)
The Curtis Center
170 S. Independence Mall West
Suite 740
West Philadelphia, PA 19106-3309
(215) 861-4900

Region IV
(AL, FL, GA, KY,* MS, NC,* SC,* TN*)
Atlanta Federal Center
61 Forsyth Street SW, Room 6T50
Atlanta, GA 30303
(404) 562-2300

Region V
(IL, IN,* MI,* MN,* OH, WI)
230 South Dearborn Street, Room 3244
Chicago, IL 60604
(312) 353-2220

Region VI
(AR, LA, NM,* OK, TX)
525 Griffin Street, Room 602
Dallas, TX 75202
(214) 767-4731 or 4736 x224

Region VII
(IA,* KS, MO, NE)
City Center Square
1100 Main Street, Suite 800
Kansas City, MO 64105
(816) 426-5861

Region VIII
(CO, MT, ND, SD, UT,* WY*)
1999 Broadway, Suite 1690
PO Box 46550
Denver, CO 80202-5716
(303) 844-1600

Region IX
(American Samoa, AZ,* CA,* HI, NV,* Northern Mariana Islands)
71 Stevenson Street, Room 420
San Francisco, CA 94105
(415) 975-4310

Region X
(AK,* ID, OR,* WA*)
1111 Third Avenue, Suite 715
Seattle, WA 98101-3212
(206) 553-5930

*These states and territories operate their own OSHA-approved job safety and health programs (Connecticut, New Jersey, and New York plans cover public employees only). States with approved programs must have a standard that is identical to, or at least as effective as, the federal standard.

Note: To get contact information for OSHA Area Offices, OSHA-approved state plans, and OSHA Consultation Projects, please visit us online at www.osha.gov or call us at (800) 321-OSHA.

www.ingramcontent.com/pod-product-compliance
Ingram Content Group UK Ltd.
Pitfield, Milton Keynes, MK11 3LW, UK
UKHW041141300926
15471UKWH00011B/86

9 780865 875210